SOUTH AFRICA

IN THE NAME
OF THE FATHER

SOUTH AFRICA

IN THE NAME
OF THE FATHER

Angus Douglas

DEFIANCE PRESS
& PUBLISHING

South Africa: In the Name of the Father

DEFIANCE **PRESS**
& PUBLISHING

ISBN-13: 978-1-959677-01-7 (Paperback)
ISBN-13: 978-1-959677-02-4 (eBook)

Published by Defiance Press and Publishing, LLC

Bulk orders of this book may be obtained by contacting Defiance Press and Publishing, LLC. www.defiancepress.com.

Public Relations Dept. – Defiance Press & Publishing, LLC
281-581-9300
pr@defiancepress.com

Defiance Press & Publishing, LLC
281-581-9300
info@defiancepress.com

DEDICATION

This book is dedicated to the memory of Alan Paton, Jan Hofmeyr, Jan Smuts, Sol Plaatje, Herman Charles Bosman, and Charles Rawden Maclean. And to all fathers, past and present. *By the way, Dad, you were right, and Ronnie Kasrils was wrong.*

ACKNOWLEDGEMENTS

Besides the people mentioned in this book, there are numerous others whose ideas and articulations I have allowed to shape my judgements about this country. I have had these sociopolitical discussions with friends and acquaintances too numerous to mention. I thank them for sharing their experiences with me, and I reserve full responsibility for the opinions expressed here, as well as for the mistruths, should sharper scholars than me discover them. I look forward to recording these conversations on my YouTube channel.

I thank my editors, Maxwell Specter and Richard Thompson, for their encouragement and editorial perspicacity. I thank Defiance Press Publishing (Mark, Dave, Cassandra, Gloria, and Kelly) for their encouragement and for helping to deliver this book to you.

For generously sharing his creativity with me over the past two decades, I thank Tim Sandham. I thank Thorsten Wedekind for generously sharing his research into South African film and television.

DISCLAIMER

The word mostly spelt *k-a-f-f-i-r*, from the Arabic term for people without religious faith, is today an unforgivable racial slur in South Africa; and referred to as "the K-word" when referenced in polite company. On the odd occasion that the word was used in the original quotation, I have changed it to something more respectful.

NOTE

I f you are interested in the philosophic underpinnings of this work, please refer to the essay *Civilization versus Tribalism* on my website *angusdouglas.co.za*.

I have endeavored to cite, or at the very least credit, all phrases that are not mine. Failure to do so is entirely my fault and I apologize unreservedly should I create the impression of passing off someone else's work as my own. I have italicized *coloured*, in acknowledgement of the problematic nature of this term that apartheid rulers used to oppress brown people.

TABLE OF CONTENTS

INTRODUCTION

If you want to keep a secret, you
must also hide it from yourself.

—*George Orwell*

I was born in 1969; for the first twenty-five years of my life I was part of a privileged minority who dominated the country. But being a sensitive and open person I found it irksome, indeed oppressive, to live in a country with such a backward, illiberal order. As a university student (1987–1990) I fell in with leftist activists; opposing a racist order seemed like the right thing to do. As a liberal I was perplexed that white South Africans were generally comfortable with their race privileges and that they saw nothing wrong with such an obviously skewed political system, one that was increasingly at odds with global trends on human rights.

Then, almost magically, the unthinkable happened and between 1990 and 1994 our white rulers conceded that South Africa belonged to all races. The transition put race relations on a sane footing. White racists can no longer abuse blacks with impunity. Indeed, by some independent studies, and by one's experience living here, racial strife is rare and racial tensions are minimal. As in most other countries, people here worry more about crime, unemployment, illegal immigration, and the cost of living, than they do about racism. Race isn't really a factor—until it is.

We live a contradiction in South Africa. Multiracialism is indeed viable, as our friendly everyday interactions with ordinary people from across the racial spectrum prove. However, African majority rule is not viable, as is proved by our daily encounters with the degradation of our state.

As a youngster my assumption was that all people are the same; if only we could loosen the shackles of a sectarian system the human spirit would flourish. After 1994 it became obvious that some shackles are important and that societies cannot flourish unless they are based on truth-telling; that the social hierarchy cannot be ordered in terms of race and nor can it be ordered in terms of antiracist ideology.

When I found myself a citizen of that nation I had idealistically striven for as a well-meaning liberal student, the very purpose of the project drained away and I wasn't sure what my role in society should be.

Then in my adulthood I became a spin-doctor. I became rather skilled at the art of spin-doctoring, which pays reasonably well. In the mid-2000s I was writing for large South African companies. Now, at last, I was back in the conversation, able to influence decision-makers, even if only from the background. I flattered myself that words matter, and as the person originating content that would land up in the mouth of a captain of industry, what I thought and what I chose to write for them mattered.

This tale is one of disillusionment with my ability to do that. Words matter only insofar as we take them seriously. What we don't say is more important than what we do say. Or rather, what we *do* is more important than what we *say*.

I am a liberal who believes that the races should coexist peaceably and prosperously. This is not up for debate. The debate is about how to do so. It is obvious to me that the majority race in this country (black Africans) have adopted—and will continue to adopt—the posture of a home-grown civilization facing off their colonial nemesis: whites. Our majoritarian electoral system means African political leaders are heavily incentivized to appeal to race solidarity.

When I wrote for captains of industry who needed to strike the right sociopolitical narrative for the country, I believed that African majority rule was viable. I felt that minority South Africans should fall in with the vision of our political masters and dedicate themselves to shoring up the credibility of their rule.

Then, during the rise of the Culture War from about 2017, I started watching a lot of YouTube videos; Jordan Peterson was very influential as were other straight shooters like Joe Rogan, Ben Shapiro, Dave Rubin, and Sam Harris.

By then I had become thoroughly disillusioned with the left-wing narrative, but I could not see a centrist alternative for South Africa. Listening to a range of conservative opinion, it struck me that it's not my job to manufacture credibility for our African elite. That's their job. My job is to tell my truth as best I can and let the chips fall where they may. I don't have to apologize for being the race I was born into; I don't have to debase the reputation of my ancestors because they're white and it's the politically correct thing to do. *I won't insult your ancestors if you don't insult mine.*

The strange thing about the Culture War is that it's not a war. The Cold War involved actual battles on the ground, as we saw play out in Angola in the 1980s, with South Africa and UNITA fighting the corner for America against the Soviet-backed MPLA government. When it comes to the current actual war, the one in Ukraine, America can at least muster bipartisan support to help Ukrainians defend their sovereignty against a fading superpower. This show of ideological coherence by the flagbearer of western values is of some comfort to minorities here.

South Africa exists in a sociopolitical twilight zone: no war and no peace. There is no actual war, but there is no ideological peace either. Everyone knows that one day the war in Ukraine will end and everything will go back to normal. In South Africa we don't have a normal to go back to, and—if you consider how hard it is for America to resolve its race conundrum—there is little chance of us finding ideological peace here.

This book flows from a sense of desolation at the hope of a rainbow nation. It offers a reality-check to liberals and a rebuke to those who hanker for the days of white supremacy, which in South Africa culminated in the absurd politics of apartheid. I grew up in the world's last white supremacist state. While our cousins overseas were rolling back segregation, the apartheid state (1948–1994) was doubling down on the idea that whites must separate from blacks and dominate them while they were at it.

Apartheid categorized people into four racial groups: black/Bantu, European/white, *coloured*, and Asian/Indian. These were sufficiently viable categories for most people to know which group they belonged to. The exception here is the designation *coloured*, which—as the word suggests—was a useful catchall for apartheid planners when they didn't know where to put people. It also referred to an established society that is some mixture of descendants of Asian slaves, West African slaves, Europeans, Khoisan, and black Africans.

Although apartheid discriminated against blacks (including *coloureds* and Indians), it was primarily aimed at oppressing indigenous Africans, who are the abiding majority in South Africa. In the racial hierarchy of apartheid, Africans were on the lowest rung, with *coloureds* and Indians somewhere in between.

Some *coloureds* and Indians identified with their oppressed African brothers during *the Struggle* against white rule (1910–1994), taking on black identity in solidarity. The ANC government has returned the favor by initially including Indians and *coloureds* in their black empowerment policy. I tend to use the term *black* in the inclusive way that our current government does. But the term is misleading. The main political contestation in this country is between indigenous Africans on the one side and the three minorities on the other. I see our main ideological contestation as: *minorities and African moderates versus the indigenous elite.* (Noting that coloureds, whose Khoisan roots make them arguably South Africa's *most* indigenous grouping, are one of the minority races.)

Africans vote overwhelmingly for the ANC or for the Economic Freedom Fighters (EFF); minorities vote overwhelmingly for the Democratic Alliance (DA) or for other center-right parties that fear African majority rule.

The EFF sell the merits of African majority chauvinism to their almost exclusively black African support base. EFF parliamentarians, who sometimes refer to themselves as *fighters*, don red overalls and domestic workers' uniforms at Parliament in solidarity with the mass of Africans who tend to occupy the lower economic strata.

Our electoral system is pure party list proportional representation. At the national level the ANC is comfortably in the majority, but at the metro and municipality level coalitions are becoming more common because no single party has the majority. This sometimes leads to an alliance between ideological opposites, the DA and the EFF. Despite these cross-ideological alliances, race is still the best predictor of how people vote. Whites, Indians, and *coloureds* overwhelmingly vote DA or to the right of the DA. Africans tend to vote ANC, with about 15% voting for the EFF. It's not too surprising that whites and Indians routinely vote against the ANC. What is more interesting is that Cape *coloureds* also do so. The DA hopes that they can build on this black support and eventually win over enough moderate Africans to defeat the ANC in a general election. To do so, they would have to find a credible African leader as their presidential candidate. As I explain in the chapter Distinct Race-cultures, Distinct Politics, this is not so easy to do.

Our white supremacist leaders in South Africa justified their racial oppression on much the same grounds as European colonists justified theirs: *We have a special duty to lead in the land of the unenlightened.*

It is tempting for conservative white South Africans to fall in with the white populism typified by Donald Trump. The thinking being: *If they* (the woke left) *are going to turn race into a weapon, then let's pick up our weapon and fight back.* That is surely not the answer, and certainly not for us here who are a minority. Race is only a weapon for those who want to retribalize politics and send us back to the Middle Ages.

Alan Paton (1903–1988), one of South Africa's most important liberal figures, described his liberalism as "a generosity of spirit, an attempt to comprehend otherness, a commitment to the rule of law, a high ideal of the worth and dignity of man, a repugnance for authoritarianism and a love of freedom."[1]

I understand that not everyone would want to emphasize these values at the expense of tradition and cultural continuity. This book is also for conservatives—those who believe in authority and common decency, who feel society needs proper boundaries to preserve the hard-won gains of civilization. Whose civilization?

Folklore has it that Gandhi said of Western Civilization, "It would be a good idea." That comment is facile. Not all cultures are equally appropriate modes of living for our modern world. There is something

---

1. Widely quoted.

called *Western Civilization*; we should honour those who bequeathed us the foundations of our liberal humanist order. These foundations include the Judeo-Christian project—with influence from the Ancient Greek and Roman civilizations. Western Civilization also brought about the Enlightenment in Europe, itself influenced by the Scientific Revolution, which began in the seventeenth century and persists to this day.

What is the West? The West used to be Western Europe and North America. Today, we could include Australia, New Zealand, and some Asian countries that lean towards the West, notably South Korea, Japan, Singapore, and, importantly, Taiwan.

Western Civilization isn't the world's only civilization but given South Africa's colonial history it is key to our political story. We are a satellite of the West—a piece of the Anglosphere in Africa—a bulwark at the southern end of the continent that was *meant* to be doing the work of Western Civilization. Our most famous company is called Anglo American, testimony to the fact that it was Brits and Americans who founded those deep-level goldmines at Johannesburg, underwriting the rise of a modern South African state.

White South Africans look to the *cultural mothership*, America and Europe, for ideological guidance and economic inspiration; black South Africans find cultural inspiration from African Americans.

In terms of our philosophy and law, it is not only the Anglophone empire that influenced us. From the Afrikaans side, Dutch-German philosophy is important, as is Roman-Dutch law, on which our legal system is founded.

We are a Roman-Dutch-Anglo outpost in an indigenous continent. So we might parody our predicament, though the parody could be considered insulting to all those people of various races and cultural backgrounds who care about their country and sincerely want to transcend the race divide in the name of human flourishing and economic success.

Indians are the least populous of the minority groups; there are only 1.54 million of them in a total of sixty million people, which is less than 3 per cent of the total. South Africa is home to some 4.6 million whites and 5.3 million *coloureds*.[2] South African Indians are the descendants of people from what is today India and Pakistan. They started arriving in 1863, but most arrived in the early 1900s as indentured servants, sent out to KwaZulu-Natal (on South Africa's eastern seaboard) to cut sugar cane. They worked off their debts soon enough and became a petit bourgeois class, mostly better off than Africans and generally better off than the relatives they left behind in India, notwithstanding the discrimination they endured under white supremacist rule. Muslim traders also immigrated to South Africa during the twentieth century. Johannesburg, Durban, and Cape Town (with its Cape Malay community) all have important Muslim communities.

The job of canary in the coalmine goes to the Jews. They once numbered some 200,000, making extraordinary contributions to art, culture, and commerce. Today there are only tens of thousands left; it's a standing joke that the traditional Jewish parts of town have become Muslim, with prominent Mosques overshadowing the Synagogues.

Islamophobia might be a thing in Europe, but not here. I got my Covid jab at a mosque run by Muslim doctors and paramedics. Muslim, Christian, or atheist, the minorities do not fear other religions as much as they dread the ruin of African rule. *Thank God for the Muslims*.

Gandhi is important in South Africa's history. He arrived here in 1893 to practice law; that same year he was ejected from a first-class railway carriage because he was black. For the next twenty-one years he fought for the rights of his people—Indians. Today it's a cause of embarrassment that the great *Mahatma* was a racist. In his struggle to

---

2. (Statista, 2021)

assert the dignity of his people and to resist the racist European colo-nial order in South Africa, Gandhi chose to distinguish his claim from that of the indigenous. He complained that, "a general belief seems to prevail in the [Natal] Colony that the Indians are a little better, if at all, than savages or the Natives of Africa."[3] He spoke out against the mixing of Indians with Africans and implied that Indians are superior to Africans because they had no *war dances* and did not drink *native beer*.[4]

Gandhi's grandson, Rajmohan Gandhi, admitted that the great man was "at times ignorant and prejudiced about South Africa's blacks."[5] (Do we listen to Gandhi or his grandson?)

The problem with Gandhi's racism cuts to the heart of our conun-drum. Yes, it is wrong to segregate ourselves and claim privileges for our civilization based only on race. Yet, it is still necessary to define the social behaviour that warrants entry into that civilization.

Some Indian figures straddle our race divide in the name of nation-building and good governance. The most important of these is Pravin Gordhan, who is now one of the ANC's most talented and commit-ted ministers. Working from within the ANC and within government, Pravin Gordhan did his best to stop the Gupta brothers (Ajay, Atul, and Rajesh) from capturing our state. From May 2009 to February 2018, President Jacob Zuma and his cronies set about selling state favors to the Guptas, a family from India. Gordhan bravely confronted Zuma supporters at the memorial of Struggle hero Ahmed Kathrada (April 2017), where he told them that being *politically radical* does not involve passing out paper bags of money.[6]

---

3. (Biswas, 2015)
4. (Biswas, 2015) It's the K-word in the original, which I changed out of respect.
5. (Biswas, 2015)
6. The reference to "paper bags of money" is from Pravin Gordhan's speech at Ahmed Kathrada's funeral in Durban, April, 2017.

Jacob Zuma sometimes dresses in traditional Zulu regalia, with the skin of the leopard featuring prominently as an aspect of royal attire. Zuma speaks and sings in *isiZulu* and seems more comfortable in his home language than in English. His supporters wore T-shirts emblazoned with the words *100 per cent Zulu Boy*. This is misleading. Zuma is not so much an ethnic tribalist as a political one. He did deals with people of any race or religion, as long as they were willing to join his patronage network. Tribalism in the modern era is less about ethnicity and language and more about patronage deals facilitated by proximity to political power. That's the tribalism destroying South Africa, not the type that is nostalgic for indigenous culture.

Urban Africans, the inheritors of the post-white-supremacist state, were meant to have transcended tribalism and made the leap to modernity. Many, I am sure, have. However, in general, our African elites have degraded our cities, plundering their resources to help their clan.

Our 1994 transition is sometimes referred to as "the overthrow of white minority rule."[7] Wrong. It was a managed handover—somewhat rushed—as ANC activists exploited the volatile times to stir up mass protest.[8] As Russia has discovered: *transition in haste, repent at leisure.*

Given the dysfunction and the ideological antagonism of our state, what are the options? What about secession? Our map, our history and our demographics do not make a great case for secession. White South Africa carved out the southern end of Africa as a unified country in 1910. On what grounds can we say that this is no longer a country and we're going to secede from it?

The Cape Independence movement seeks to unite *coloured* and white against the Africanist majoritarian project. That's not quite how

---

7. (Harber, 2020) Harber quotes *The Wall Street Journal* using this phrasing.
8. Journalist Rian Malan has written extensively on the violent protests during the transition, suggesting that Mandela's attacks on FW de Klerk during that time were not justified by the evidence.

they describe it, but that's what their secession movement (sometimes called *CapeXit*) amounts to.[9] *Coloureds* are more populous than Indians, and their concentration in the Cape Province makes them important for those who plot secession. In the Cape, *coloureds* are 40% of the total population, with whites at 16%; the remainder are mostly black African. This means that the two minorities can collaborate to dominate provincial and local government in the Cape. As a result of this, many people from the minorities are moving there.

Short of sparking a civil war, I cannot see *coloured* and white claiming the Cape as their own country that will forever remain immune to African majority rule. Besides, even if the Cape were to secede and minorities from other parts of the country flocked there, the loss of expertise would cause economic collapse in South Africa, and the Cape would be inundated with economic refugees. We could solve our political crisis, but not without creating a humanitarian one. No, we must fight this one from wherever we find ourselves in the country.

Further, as I write this, the Cape is slowly but surely becoming a province demographically dominated by black Africans. Economic refugees come from the Eastern Cape, one of South Africa's poorer provinces, and from other African countries. This is not a new story. Even during the height of apartheid, Africans from neighbouring countries were desperate to enter this country in search of paid work. White supremacy was not good for African pride, but it wasn't too bad for African job opportunities. Successful minority enclaves in Africa will always be inundated with economic refugees from dysfunctional African states.

This country was built on white initiative and cheap black labour—a nasty co-dependency that did not disappear with the end of

---

9. As of writing (October 2022) this secession movement does not enjoy widespread support from coloureds and whites. However, there are growing calls from minorities for more federalism to give them some security from a collapsing central state.

white rule. Our only political hope is that a multiracial bourgeoisie, led by moderate Africans and minorities, prevails against a chauvinistic African political elite.

Why, after all the efforts made to integrate, and after white supremacy has been thoroughly rubbished in all respectable quarters, has the world become so hyped about race and racism? *Racism* used to refer to an irrational hatred of black people, a *negro-phobia* at being close to a black skin or touching Afro-hair. It also used to refer to white supremacism, the belief that whites have a special destiny to dominate blacks. Both of those positions are now taboo.

The ideological battle to defeat this type of racism has been won. Anyone who argues that there is value in *negro-phobia* and white supremacy is shamed from polite society. In the wake of the Holocaust, racism became taboo in the West, a taboo that eventually broke the spell of white supremacy in Africa.

Yet today, with actual racism on the decline, *racist* has become a slur to defame your enemies. According to the anti-racist religion, *systemic racism* is evidenced by a general fact of unequal outcomes between the races, be it in prison numbers, board-level representation, or mortgage approvals. By this definition, there is indeed still a lot of racism in the world and will be for centuries to come.

The neuroscientist and podcast host Sam Harris explains why our new catchall definition of racism is so troubling:

> human populations have lived apart for thousands and thousands of years, so they're going to differ genetically. Then you have differences of culture layered on top of that. Take Norwegians and Japanese. You can look at people and tell that they didn't come from Norway or didn't come from Japan. These people are different, they have different cultures, different languages. It would be an absolute miracle if everything

we cared about were at the same mean level in those groups … To say mere discovery of difference is a sign of ethical pathology or needs to be politically catastrophic—that just sets you up for an endless round of conflict.[10]

Rian Malan, a cool chronicler of our predicament and the author of the era-defining *My Traitor's Heart* (1990), makes a similar point to Harris: "I am going to call it the beautiful idea. Because it's beautiful in a way—but also dangerous. The beautiful idea holds that all humans are born with identical gifts and should turn out to be clones of one another in a just society. Conversely, any situation in which disparity survives is in itself proof of injustice."[11] Our culture is befuddled by a beautiful idea that few respectable commentators are willing to challenge. Why? Because in doing so we look ugly.

What's the solution? The first step is to acknowledge race and the abiding fact that we still strongly associate, both politically and socially, with people of our own race. The next step is to admit that you cannot build a country out of non-racial individuals. That was South Africa's hope—*hope dies last.*[12]

The solutions to our crisis are not at hand. But we can at least inch our way out of the dark by ending our denials about race and reframing our situation in ways that do not violate our intuitions on the subject.

South Africa has good weather, good minerals, a progressive constitution, the goodwill of major powers, and decent infrastructure. We are also *blessed* with diversity. Or, cursed with diversity, depending on how you look at it. Is human diversity a good thing? That's what the left says when they tell us to celebrate diversity. *Celebrate* is too strong a word. Rather, in the immortal words of Rodney King, *can we, can we*

---

10. (Waking Up with Sam Harris, 2018)
11. (Malan, 2021)
12. I refence here Alexander Dubcek's account of dealing with the Soviet leadership.

all get along?

Our modern *religions*—Marxism and liberal humanism—were meant to delete race from the conversation. They failed. In South Africa white communists joined with African communists to fight white supremacy, as did white liberals join with African liberals. Liberals and communists succeeded in ending white rule, but they failed in establishing an ideology that would transcend race.

During the apartheid years, Afrikaners liked to compare themselves to Jews, *a chosen minority whose Godly destiny it was to rule over this promised land.* South Africa's founding father Jan Smuts compared the Boers to the Jews, stating that they both deserved "historic justice."[13]

The Afrikaners had their own *holocaust* in the second part of the Anglo-Boer War (1899–1902). After British forces captured the Boer capital of Pretoria in June 1900, instead of surrendering, many Boer leaders—including Jan Smuts—began a hit-and-run guerrilla campaign against a lumbering British army. The British response was to destroy Boer supply lines, which meant burning down their farms and putting their women, children, and servants into concentration camps. Poor sanitation led to the deaths of some thirty thousand Boer children and women (but mostly children), as well as thousands of their African servants. The loss was borne by the Boers of the Transvaal and the Orange Free State, some 50% of whose children died in the camps.

Although Britain's sin was more one of omission than commission, Afrikaner nationalists nursed this grievance and never forgave the British for using *coloureds* and Africans to do some of their dirty work. By some accounts, the British used 100,000 blacks to assist their war effort, 30,000 of whom were armed.[14] In January 1902, in an earlier echo of oppressed South Africans appealing to English liberals for support,

---

13. (Dubow, 2019)
14. (Marks, 2001, p. 219) Marks cites numerous reliable sources for these numbers.

Jan Smuts wrote to the British journalist WT Stead, who was sympathetic to the Boer cause. In the letter Smuts criticized Britain's "baneful policy" of using "Native and Coloured people as armed combatants … in thousands."[15] According to Smuts, "these fiends committed horrible atrocities on peaceful women and children—almost as many have perished at the hands of barbarians in this war, by the connivance of British officers, as were done to death by Dingaan and Moselekatze."[16]

What was Smuts going on about? Were the British getting blacks to do their killing and their dying for them? Thousands of blacks from both sides of the conflict died uncelebrated deaths in the Anglo-Boer War; hence the politically correct renaming of it to the *South African War*. For a brief period during colonialism, armed Africans and coloureds, backed by the British Empire, had their chance to get one over the bullying Boers. Smuts believed that *involving the coloured races* in a white man's war was a *Frankenstein Monster* that would lead to an *eventual debacle of society*, causing *South Africa to relapse into barbarism.*[17]

The bitterness of the war poisoned our politics and indirectly led to apartheid, which thoroughly codified white domination. Not exactly the type of *historic justice* Smuts had in mind.

Unlike Israel, which has achieved a stable and sustainable state founded on the principles of Jewish self-determination, white South Africans could not secure themselves a long-term state. Our white-run state ended in 1994; now many of us are essentially a stateless people in a declining African country. Smuts's warning from 1895, if politically incorrect for our times, has a ring of truth to it: "Unless the white race closes its ranks in this country, its position will soon

---

15. (Marks, 2001, p. 216)
16. (Marks, 2001, p. 216) Slightly paraphrased from the original; *Moselekatze* is now spelt *Mzilikazi*.
17. (Marks, 2001, p. 217)

become untenable in the face of that overwhelming [African] majority of prolific barbarism."[18] This sort of talk is now taboo, but there is a kernel of truth worth retrieving from Smuts's dark vision. Something like this: *unless minorities and moderate Africans make a united stand against chauvinistic African posturing, the country is finished.*

---

18. (Marks, 2001, p. 215)

WE HAVE A LOOTING PROBLEM

The prophecies of this book have come to pass even before I could finish it. As I write (July 2021), the country is held hostage by looters who burn down factories, destroy businesses, and help themselves to flat-screen TVs and other desirable goods. All (*almost all*) of them are Africans, some of them are even middle class, arriving to loot in those luxury vehicles that were meant to confer dignity. Our world culture tells them they are victims of white sins and will ever be thus. The leftist ideology that sanctifies the indigenous as unconditionally innocent is working its evil in far-off South Africa. They are the children who must never grow up.

I take a drive around my hometown and witness scenes from *Zombie Apocalypse*: parents and children manning barricades armed with cricket bats, paintball guns, and hunting rifles. One guy gives me a friendly wave from his camping chair, hunting rifle resting up against him. The mood is not quite as Coetzee had it in *Waiting for the Barbarians* (intellectuals inhabit their own universe of reconstituted meaning); no—it's friendly and communal. I am on their side; I salute them for protecting us from looting hordes. I see African people in white and Indian areas and am relieved that they're left to go about their business and are not victims of racial hatred.

This was never about racial hatred, and it's not about racial hatred now. It's about the truth, which is that if you patronize a class of people as the sacred victims of a global conspiracy, and then get them to rule your country, you're in deep trouble. I see it playing out in boardrooms, in politics, and in everyday interactions. The country is breaking, but not because of looting and State Capture; it's breaking because every day in a thousand meetings and conferences across the country, we wear a mask. The mask covers the fact that it's shameful and humiliating to put someone in a position of expertise who is not capable of it, and who needs to be babied by real experts in the background. Healing this country means taking off the mask and telling each other the truth.

What's happening at the last line of defense when hordes of people attack? How do we respond and who do we trust to protect us?

There are a few extraordinary and troubling things about that week in July 2021, when order collapsed in parts of the country and hordes of people went on a looting and burning rampage. The chaos was sparked when former president Jacob Zuma was jailed for contempt of court after he refused to appear before the Zondo Commission of Inquiry into State Capture.

It seems that pro-Zuma agitators and disaffected ANC people, together with opportunistic criminals, used social media platforms (particularly WhatsApp groups) to foment an insurrection. The unrest began in KwaZulu-Natal on the evening of 9 July; it then spread to parts of Gauteng on 11 July and subsided by 18 July.

Ordinary people became swept up in the excitement of getting something for nothing, and rushed to join the looting spree. Television images showed a traffic jam of vehicles: looters driving to shopping centres and factories to help themselves to electronic goods, furniture, clothing, and whatever else they could lay their hands on. In one of its articles the *Daily Maverick*, a news site, showed a picture with the caption: "Looters packing their BMW with furniture in Springfield on 13 July 2021 in Durban." Two days after that picture was taken, I joined a voluntary clean-up operation at that exact place in Durban. It was clear that not all looters had arrived in a BMW. A food store had been looted; half-eaten food now littered the road. The apologists who put the looting down to hungry people desperate after months of Covid lockdowns were not entirely wrong. Many in South Africa go to bed hungry; here was the evidence that this hunger had been part of their motivation to loot.

During that clean-up with friends and strangers, I was overcome with emotion. There was shame in the air. Our liberal ideal had been degraded.

A young African man, Ndumiso, was one of the clean-up volunteers. I questioned him about the *unrest*. Did he know anyone who had joined the looting spree? And why did they do it? Ndumiso was both dignified and truthful. Yes, some of his friends had joined. He pointed to the large retail clothing store, Mr Price, and told me that his friends who worked there were the very ones who had looted it. They also looted alcohol, Ndumiso told me, and now they were hungover and jobless. Ndumiso had lost his job because of Covid; the clean-up, although unpaid, gave him something constructive to do.

To my shame, when my white friends and I gathered for a Facebook pic at the end of the day, we didn't invite Ndumiso into our circle. There he stood a few metres from us, possibly feeling excluded by a group of whites. Perhaps not, but I felt bad that I hadn't brought him in, excusing it for the moment as a Covid-distancing precaution.

What is inclusion? A white couple had brought their children along to help with the clean-up. One of them was African, a good-looking youngster of about ten or eleven. I assumed he was their adopted child. The parents were clearly upset, but were doing what good people do: channeling confusing emotions into productive activity; creating some order out of chaos.

We were joined by municipal workers who arrived with large garbage trucks to cart away the debris. A middle-aged Indian man oversaw the team, which included a handful of African workers. His kind demeanor and the prayer beads around his neck made me think he was religious.

This gentle, good-humored man humbled me to my core. There was racial tension in the air between Indians and Africans; he artfully transcended all that, cajoling us with heart and humor. Our country hangs by a thread—a thread of kindness shown by a truck driver with a dot on his forehead and a string of prayer-beads around his neck.

In the aftermath of the *unrest*, a euphemistic term we thought had died with apartheid, the question of race emerged not so much from the perspective of *black versus white* but *Indian versus African*. That was the real racial frontline of the story. Durban is known for having a large Indian population—the largest outside of India, we are sometimes told.

In January 1949, in one of the most serious massacres during apartheid and the least publicized, Africans attacked Indians, killing dozens of people—perhaps as many as a hundred. Women were raped and Indian shops were looted and destroyed. By some accounts the Durban riots, as they were called, amounted to an *anti-Indian pogrom*.[19] Whatever the racial features of the strife there was an economic element to it too. Indians are successful traders and shopkeepers. The Africans in KwaZulu-Natal (who happen to be largely Zulu) make up the poor masses who buy from these shops, sometimes on credit. Like history's pogroms against the Jews, the pogrom against the Indians in

---

19. (Wikipedia, 2022)

Durban was partly fomented by economic jealousy.

A surprising feature of those 1949 Durban riots is that apparently some white women encouraged Africans in their rampage, exhorting them to "hit the *coolies*."[20]

The 2021 riots were different from those 1949 riots. Indians were reasonably well-prepared and some used firearms to protect their property; this time no white women were heard encouraging Africans to attack Indians—not even on social media. Official reports put the final death toll at over 350 people; most were black African.

The *Daily Maverick* quoted KwaZulu-Natal premier Sihle Zikalala commenting at the time, "The vast majority of the killings took place in KwaZulu-Natal and were as a result of looters being crushed in the frenzy for stolen goods, or fighting with each other over the same goods."[21]

A few days before the clean-up I went on a foraging mission to the sprawling India area of Phoenix. There was an eerie warzone feel in the air. Eerie and exciting.

It was the burnt-out cars and trashed roads, the chemical smell of burning factories. The old Indian guy we gave a lift. He was proud that his people had defended themselves—that they had taken the fight to the Africans … or words to that effect.

In the white areas, roadblocks were being manned by middle-class families. Men predominated at the frontline, but I saw women and children joining in. South Africa has been spatially developed with this sort of event in mind. We are built and financed to absorb the shock of a horde of rioters.[22] Sometimes, the shock-absorbers are racial.

---

20. (Wikipedia, 2022) The original source for this is *The Deadly Ethnic Riot* (2001), Donald Horowitz, University of California Press. I did not confirm the citation in the original but assume it to be accurate. *Coolie* is a racial slur used against Indians that is thankfully becoming less common.
21. (Erasmus, 2021)
22. South Africa has something called SASRIA (special riot cover insurance).

White supremacy is still evident in our town planning: the massive Indian sprawl of Phoenix was the buffer to protect those coastal white suburbs from the poor African areas inland.

I was staying with my elderly mother and her husband in Umhlanga, the popular holiday spot just ten minutes' drive north of Durban. Although predominantly white, Umhlanga is multiracial, as are the suburbs around it. I noticed that the roadblock defenders were also multiracial: white and Indian defenders backed by African-manned private security. This proved a highly effective defensive arrangement against a horde. Closer to Durban, I went through a few ragged roadblocks. Here I witnessed not only political decay in South Africa, but also signs that the opioid epidemic, imported from *Empire America*, had degraded those defending our civilization. Poor whites, some quite clearly down and out addicts, were manning roadblocks and confronting Durban's ANC city officials who came to disarm them. By some accounts these benighted white defenders racially abused the city officials. Either way, they were not persuaded to abandon their arms or their position. Meanwhile, cries of *Allahu akbar!* (God is great!) from Muslim defenders were reassuring to scared whites.

You felt safe during that week of looting. That was the strangest part of it. I felt safer sleeping in my childhood home for that week than I had in years. Roadblocks and boundaries work.

In the Indian area I noticed that Africans were free to go about their business; the atmosphere was calm and relaxed. Shops were emptying out fast, there were long queues—people milling about outdoors—but no sense of panic. I was pleasantly surprised to get my hands on some generous pieces of mutton.

What was going on at those roadblocks? There were some complaints of racial profiling, but not many. It's common cause that middle-class Africans living in white areas found themselves being protected by minority-led units backed by paid African auxiliaries. Some middle-class Africans joined the looting, as the television reports show, but many Africans found themselves on the same side as the armed whites and Indians calling the shots.

What shots?

One of the most worrying narratives emanating from some on the left was of a *Phoenix massacre*, whereby Indians supposedly massacred thirty-eight unarmed Africans at the border between the poor African area of Inanda and the Indian area Phoenix (where I went to forage for food).

The *Daily Maverick*, a newspaper, quoted an anonymous employee at the local morgue: "I don't know how many people have to die to constitute a massacre, but whatever name you want to give it—there was an exponentially high number of deaths of mainly black [African] people."[23] This piece appeared slightly differently in the print edition from the online version. It seemed an editor had wanted to make something out of the massacre, with little more to go on than an anonymous quotation.

This anonymous quotation was the only evidence I've come across indicating any kind of a *racial massacre*. Was it an example of a faulty Africanist narrative infecting newsroom ethics as it did the *Sunday Times* during the State Capture years? (I explore this in the chapter Why 'Nothing Has Changed in South Africa'.)

Is it wise to pick at the sore of a race massacre? Even if Indians did kill Africans, what choice did they have but to defend their property against marauding hordes? In that situation it is inevitable that some defenders would overreach.

I spoke to a modern-day echo of Charles Rawden Maclean, whose reflections conclude this moral tale. Clint Maclean (no direct relation)

---

23. (Daily Maverick, 2021)

is a self-styled humanitarian who wears his red hair in dreadlocks and feeds starving people. He was at the frontline because he had some people to feed.

A few days after the mayhem, I caught up with him at an outdoor coffee hangout by the beach. He had had a few close calls, menacing scenes set in the fading winter light of a South African township.

His assessment is that some defenders went too far. He was not talking about Phoenix, but about other frontlines he had come across and stories he had heard. But he talked approvingly of a tough-guy friend of his at first complaining about being called into action before stopping himself, muttering, "I'm built for this shit."

While we were chatting, Clint got into an argument with an acquaintance, a pilot on his way to run supplies into some unstable Middle Eastern country. Clint accused the pilot of being callous about black lives. Clint was not against self-defense, but he didn't like the macho swagger of some of the defenders.

Newspapers stretched euphemism to deceit, calling the unrest *protest action*.[24] The government turned to the handy *insurrection*. Everyone could see that this was a looting frenzy, with sabotage thrown in for good measure. The leader of the opposition Democratic Alliance (DA), John Steenhuisen, visited Phoenix Police Station soon after the unrest subsided.

He gave a press conference where he criticized ANC bigwigs for not visiting Phoenix and finding out the truth for themselves. The footage of his speech is revealing. Here to show support for the citizens of Phoenix in defending their lives and property against a lawless mob, he draws a distinction between the Phoenix residents and ... he pauses searching for the right term, before blurting out, "the looting

---

24. *Business Day* used the term.

fraternity."[25] It's a moment of no-nonsense Trump-like clarity for calling the crap for what it is. Amazingly, I saw no backlash against this term; of course Steenhuisen has every right to use it in drawing a distinction between civilians and those who would act like barbarians.

There is an important caveat to the July 2021 unrest. It was rife in areas of large Zulu populations, like KwaZulu-Natal and parts of Gauteng, but it didn't ignite across the other eight provinces, where *amaZulu* (Zulus) do not constitute a majority. *AmaZulu* is South Africa's largest ethnolinguistic group. They constitute about a fifth of our total population, and *isiZulu* is spoken by a quarter of South Africans.[26] *isiZulu* is a powerful language in South Africa, as Jacob Zuma proved. It's a pastoral language that *uShaka* repurposed for his military ambitions, welding disparate clans into a common tongue.

Many of those looting WhatsApp groups were communicating in *isiZulu*. In Gauteng, there were isolated incidents of looting, and examples of ordinary Africans in townships like Soweto doing what whites and Indians were doing in KwaZulu-Natal, defending their property against hordes.

The extensive journalistic coverage of this country shows that from 1994, the looting fraternity has been slowly but surely taking over the state. For nine years President Jacob Zuma, in league with the Gupta brothers from India, conducted a white-collar looting spree that cost the country hundreds of billions of rands. And then when ordinary people got in on the act, the police and military were unable to protect our factories and shopping centres. It was mostly left to civilians and private security companies to do so. Ironies of ironies, it was the reactionary minorities who defended the state in this time of crisis. The state itself was nowhere to be seen, because it cannot decide whether it

---

25. I saw it on a YouTube video covering the press conference.
26. (Galal, 2022)

is a looting patronage machine or a grownup state that cares about the destiny of the country.[27]

For decades, the global movement of anti-racism has shamed us for expressing intuitions and observations on this subject. Here's one example: *Africans are lovely people, but generally speaking, they struggle to build viable nations.* You're not allowed to say that in a boardroom or any meeting of high-minded intent. Now that we're defending our neighborhoods from hordes, we're freer to reject the ideas of our intelligentsia and fall back on our intuitions, which have been right all along. It turns out that groups are different. How obvious. That's what diversity means and that's why it's a challenge.

It's a shame that white South Africa will be remembered for institutionalized white supremacy. In the nineteenth century a white administration in the Cape gave educated and landed Africans an equal vote. In the twentieth century we followed the dead-end path of white domination. And now we follow the well-worn path of African post-liberation collapse.

In April 2022, after flooding in KwaZulu-Natal, government promised aid for residents. Steenhuisen took this as an opportunity to tell President Ramaphosa, "Do not guarantee people that relief aid will not be stolen when you know that your party has a looting problem."[28]

Houston ... we have a looting problem! Our civilization is being looted in front of our eyes. Drive around our towns, stick your finger out the window, and take a read on the trust levels. They're low; in inverse proportion to the height of the security walls. Drive around our cities and you'll see that big business has either moved out or turned their building into a fortress. And the people running big business are

---

27. There was some police and military anti-looting action, although it was sporadic and ineffective at stopping the serious plunder of the first few days and in protecting suburbs like Phoenix from invasion; this was left to residents and private security.
28. (Dlamini, 2022)

living in compounds and enclaves, their money overseas, anything to decouple from a deteriorating state and a country with no meaning. The European *race-culture* (my preferred term to *race*) was not quite sure what it was doing when it surrendered power in 1994.

Nelson Mandela was meant to transcend our race problems. As president, he did indeed transcend our racial divide and put the country on the path of peace. But his is a different world to my white world.[29] Mandela was wrong to launch an insurrectionary army in 1961, *uMkhonto we Sizwe* (Spear of the Nation). There was still a legal order; the apartheid state was not rounding up people and shooting them like in Nazi Germany.

Although I did then, I would not vote for Nelson Mandela today. I would not vote for any of the presidents our black majority have served up. None of them is a patch on Jan Smuts. I trust someone like Helen Zille or John Steenhuisen to defend the rules-based society. But I don't trust the ANC to do so, nor do I trust our African elite to provide the necessary leadership to steer the ship of state.

Our meaning will come from minorities taking back some agency for the destiny of the country, whereby we enjoy representation at the top table of national government. Africans can run the country, but not without our help.

---

29. I saw Nelson Mandela addressing an ANC women's group in Durban. He made a joke about wife abuse. Something about the one wife being jealous because her husband beat the other wife more. The largely female audience was amused.

HOW LONG WILL SOUTH AFRICA SURVIVE?

We are awash with anecdotes of state decline. Friends and family around the dinner table relate horror stories about corrupt, incompetent government officials who must be bribed to do their jobs. The newspapers overflow with tales of state incompetence and venality.

But what about the experts who have dedicated their lives to uncovering the machinations of the state? What do they say?

There've been some important books on South Africa's post-apartheid decline: *How Long Will South Africa Survive?* (RW Johnson); *What's Gone Wrong? On the Brink of a Failed State* (Alex Boraine); *After the Party: Corruption, the ANC, and South Africa's Uncertain Future* (Andrew Feinstein); *Pale Native* (Max du Preez); *Gods, Spies and Lies: Finding South Africa's Future Through its Past* (John Matisonn); *The President's Keepers: Those Keeping Zuma in Power and out of Prison* (Jacques Pauw); *After Dawn: Hope After State Capture* (Mcebisi Jonas); to mention but some.

There are also three works by Frans Cronje on the prospects of the nation; his most recent is *The Rise or Fall of South Africa: Latest*

Scenarios (2020). Cronje was CEO of the South African Institute of Race Relations (IRR) for eight years before stepping down in 2021. The IRR is an independent research and policy organization with a commitment to classical liberal values: free enterprise, law and order, property rights ... that sort of thing. Cronje's books are well-researched and point to the ANC's inability to hold it together. I came across an Amazon review that puts Cronje's analysis in an interesting frame. Richard (surname unknown) writes:

> I believe this is the third book Frans Cronje has authored; I've read all three. His style was initially novel and made for an interesting read, but sadly, in my opinion, this is one book too many. There are only so many ways one can define how and why South Africa is becoming or has become a failed state, and Cronje and others of similar mind have already beaten them to death ... More useful at this juncture would be some innovative and workable ideas for those hapless people left behind as to what can be done to stem the rot and restore a stable and civilized order to South Africa.[30]

That's why I wrote this book. There are plenty of places for readers to find the facts about African majority misrule in South Africa. We now need to understand what was wrong with our framing of white rule that it heralded this disaster. Maybe then we can start to fix it.

The books I mention above from these various authors have a common theme. In the immediate aftermath of white rule, inspired by the Mandela vision, well-meaning South Africans from across the racial divide collaborate to build a caring and capable state. The *post-apartheid spring* falters at the end of Mandela's reign in 1999. Mbeki's presidency (1999–2008) puts Africanist ideology back on the table as multiracialism declines. Politically connected Africans replace

---

30. (Richard, 2020)

committed social democrats from the minority races, pushing them out of important state jobs and blocking their anti-corruption efforts.

Mbeki's faults were masked by his good macroeconomic decision-making, and by robust global demand for South Africa's commodities. Under President Zuma (2009–2018) there was no mask for ANC failings; things went from worrying to utterly disillusioning.

Helped by high commodity prices, Mbeki succeeded in his broad macro-economic goals. South Africa's economy grew by 40 per cent in the first decade of the millennium, but there were worrying signs. He presided over a corrupt arms deal, took an anti-science stance on Aids, did not confront the tyrannical Mugabe in Zimbabwe, and failed to adequately invest in generation for the state-owned power utility, Eskom.[31]

Zuma took over just after the global financial crisis in 2008. In the decade leading up to 2020, our economy grew by only 16 per cent. Contrast this to apartheid rule: in the 1960s, the economy grew 71 per cent; in the 1970s, it grew 36 per cent; in the 1980s, 19 per cent; and in the 1990s, 17 per cent.[32] Even at the height of international action against the white state, it still managed better growth than in Zuma's time.

The ANC finally got rid of Zuma just before the expiration of his presidential term limit. I heaved a sigh of relief when the pro-business Cyril Ramaphosa was made ANC president; and then panicked again when it dawned on me that Ramaphosa had done a last-minute deal with David Mabuza, effectively delivering the deputy presidency of the country to Mabuza. Evidence suggests that Mabuza is as corrupt as Zuma, and appears to be even more ruthless than Zuma in bumping

---

31. A 2021 article in *The Economist* references "a Harvard study" by which Mbeki's "abject handling of the Aids plague cost at least 330,000 lives." (*The Economist*, 2021)
32. (Whitfield, 2020)

off those who would report him. [33]

What's the main thing wrong with South Africa that the ANC can't fix? Depending on whether you count discouraged work-seekers, South Africa's unemployment rate is between 30 and 40 per cent (the world's highest, according to some independent studies).

Unemployment does not overly affect professionals and skilled entrepreneurs, who can emigrate or perhaps live here in a secure enclave earning money online. That's me. Yet this is a rarefied reality. In South Africa, twenty to thirty million people live on less than the upper-bound poverty line of $90 per month.

Mcebisi Jonas is a leading ANC light who has tried to get to the bottom of what is behind the decline of South Africa's state. (Jonas famously turned down a six hundred-million-rand Gupta bribe to become finance minister.) In *After Dawn: Hope After State Capture* (2019) he details the "political-economy deal" of 1994 that divvied the country up into four interest groups: *white wealth*; *organised labour*; *poor and unemployed*; *new black elite*.[34]

Jonas says these interest groups were each promised a dividend: workers' rights for organised labour; grants for the poor; and guarantees to whites that they could keep their capital. So far so good—but what about Jonas' class, the new black elite? What's their dividend?

Here Jonas drops a bombshell, telling us that the ambitions of the new black elite were "placated" through "state-business patronage networks … rents in the form of preferential ownership and procurement schemes."[35] What's wrong with South Africa and why are so many people poor and unemployed? Read this paragraph again. The people who are meant to be driving growth and dynamism in the economy—the new African elite—are living off rents and patronage networks.

33. Ferial Haffajee described him as such in an online editorial.
34. (Jonas, 2019)
35. (Jonas, 2019)

In response to the Zuma-Gupta (*Zupta*) capture of our state, a group of South African academics put together a report in 2017, titled *The Betrayal of the Promise*. In the report, they stated that the media "conceive of Zuma and his allies as a criminal network that has captured the state." The academics argued that this was true on the surface but that it obscured a deeper truth: "This approach, which is unfortunately dominant, obscures the existence of a political project at work to repurpose state institutions to suit a constellation of rent-seeking networks that have been constructed and now span the symbiotic relationship between the constitutional and the shadow state."[36]

Even with Zuma gone, we still live with the same shadow state, which predated Zuma's presidency and will continue without him. In 2007, then-ANC secretary general, Kgalema Motlanthe said: "This rot is across the board … Almost every project is conceived because it offers opportunities for certain people to make money."[37] The rot he was talking about is the ANC's *cadre-deployment* policy, which *The Economist* describes as: "ANC party members get jobs on the basis of factional fealty rather than merit … These appointees steer projects towards chosen 'tenderpreneurs', who in turn donate to the party."[38]

The same article notes: "Black Economic Empowerment, a policy that incentivizes firms to give equity to black investors or business to black-owned suppliers, has created a new generation of Randlords with more political acumen than entrepreneurial talent."[39] President Ramaphosa is a billionaire because white-owned companies gave him shares to sit on their boards.[40] The rumor is that he was meant to have shared some of his stash with the ANC, but didn't. His wealth and

36. (Harber, 2020, p. 147) Harber cites the report.
37. (*The Economist*, 2021)
38. (*The Economist*, 2021) Motlanthe was president of South African for a few months in late 2008, early 2009.
39. (*The Economist*, 2021)
40. He is a billionaire in rand terms; he is worth about half a billion US dollars.

that of his brother-in-law, Patrice Motsepe, probably helped him clinch some last-minute deals at the ANC electoral conference held at the Nasrec exhibition centre and win the vote for ANC president in 2017, succeeding Zuma as party head.

In 2007, there was already a shadow state as Motlanthe attested. It only became more brazen under Zuma. From the start of African majority rule, our bureaucracy and state machinery has become *tribalized*: patronage and personal reciprocity above state-building.

This is the damning failure of our African political elite, who are unable to create a credible political order. African elites in countries to the north have the same problem. Journalist John Matisonn cites Moeletsi Mbeki (the ex-president's brother) on the subject:

> His reading told him that elsewhere in Africa after independence, leaders kept power if they kept urban political elites fed. The elite tried to live at levels comparable with those of the middle and upper classes in the West, at the expense of infrastructure investment. Paying lip service to development, they undertook "half-hearted, loss-making industrialisation projects that were not supported by the necessary technical and managerial development."[41]

What happens when the ruling elite pay lip service to development and live at unsustainable levels of consumption at the expense of infrastructure investment? State decline. It's the common postcolonial problem of urban elites unable or unwilling to build strong institutions of state. Political scientists have various terms for the phenomenon of a bureaucratic class who use their office for personal gain at the expense of a functional state: *rent-seeking, neopatrimonialism, clientelism, venality, prebendalism*. The renowned scholar Richard A. Joseph uses

---

41. (Mattison, 2015, p. 410)

the term *prebendalism* to describe Nigerian politics, where government officials share in the spoils of state revenue. It's the same problem that benighted France's *ancien régime.* As Francis Fukuyama puts it: "A modern France could not arise until venal officeholding was replaced by impersonal, merit-based bureaucracy."[42]

A modern Africa will not emerge until the same is achieved here. In South Africa, the African middle-class simply does not have the skills and wherewithal—perhaps not the intention either—to turn the ship of state around. They need private business to help them do it; but private business is run mainly by whites and Indians, who are not committed to the project of indigenous redress and anti-colonialism. Why should they be? Antiracism and anti-colonialism are failed ideologies that are based on a false assumption, which is that foreign rule was ruinous for indigenous Africans. The fact is that ordinary Africans had access to more economic opportunities under colonialism than they have under postcolonialism.

There is an ocean of capital sloshing around the world's financial markets. If a country wants to attract some of it, all it needs to do is guarantee a reasonable return for the owners. For various reasons, African countries are generally unable to guarantee those returns, so they miss out on growth. By contrast, in colonial times investors could be reassured. As Niall Ferguson puts it: "Investing in such [developing] economies is risky. They tend to be far away and more prone to economic, social, and political crises. But the extension of the empire into the less developed world had the effect of reducing such risks by imposing directly, or indirectly, some form of European rule."[43]

Investors don't like economies of patronage and prebendalism and so have tended to steer clear of Africa in the postcolonial age. Ferguson

---

42. (Fukuyama, 2012, p. 349)
43. (Ferguson, 2011)

points out that in 1913, 63 per cent of foreign direct investment went to developing countries; by 1996, it was only 28 per cent. In 1913, 25 per cent of the world's stock of capital was invested in countries whose per-capita-GDP was a fifth or less than that of the US. In 1997, only 5 per cent of the world's stock of capital was being invested in such countries.[44]

Ferguson reports that, today, Britain's per-capita-GDP is roughly twenty times that of Zambia; at the end of the colonial period (1955), it was only seven times greater. As he puts it, "It has been since independence that the gap between the colonizer and the ex-colony has become a gulf. The same is true of nearly all former colonies in sub-Saharan Africa, with the notable exception of Botswana."[45] These financial facts suggest that after colonialism, Africa went from being seen as an economic and geopolitical opportunity to becoming a humanitarian cause: not to be invested in but to be saved.

Why does anticolonialism still dominate the discourse about Africa? The discourse serves a purpose. It exaggerates colonial wrong to provide cover for underperforming elites.

Ideological cover is what Julius Malema excels at. His EFF is on the hard Africanist edge of the ANC. In 2013, Malema, who was then ANC Youth League supremo, fell out with President Zuma and broke away, along with fellow disaffected radicals, to form the EFF. Instead of humbling himself to the ANC brand, he created an Africanist brand of his own, borrowing the Cuban Revolution (1953) manifesto for a creed. For the EFF, *economic freedom* does not mean the freedom to pursue opportunity unhindered by an interfering state; it means taking from whites and giving to Africans.

The EFF claim to be against *white monopoly capital*. That's

---

44. (Ferguson, 2011)
45. (Ferguson, 2011)

only half true. They're against whites and Indians, regardless of their capital. Malema has a personal vendetta against the minister of public enterprises, Pravin Gordhan, whom the EFF goads by using his second name, *Jamnadas*, sometimes corrupting or misspelling it, making a nasty point about the fact that Gordhan is Indian and not black African. The minorities fear that one day Malema will return to the ANC to lead the party and the country.

ANC policy is to build a developmental state that protects the indigent, promotes black enterprise, and creates decent jobs. In reality the ANC undermines these aims with its meddling in state-owned enterprises and their confused policy, a cross between European welfarism and African indigenization.

Your sensitive white liberal is quite likely to be considering life abroad (if they haven't already moved), engaging in South African politics from the comfort of their Facebook account. Respected journalist and author RW Johnson sums up the gloom we feel: "South Africa can either choose to have an ANC government or it can have a modern industrial economy. It cannot have both."[46]

What if we exchange his term *ANC government* for *African rule*? Johnson would be called a racist for doing so, yet it's only logical to suppose that the ANC is our best shot at African rule. Another African party (e.g., the EFF, or Inkatha) is unlikely to do any better than the ANC. What Johnson is truly pessimistic about is not the ANC *per se*, but African majority rule.[47]

The truth is that almost all the parts of South Africa that qualify it as a modern industrial democracy are held together by minority

---

46. (Johnson, 2015)
47. Even Johnson, an ardent critic of African rule here, is disingenuous about the situation. He points to Botswana as a counter example to the failure of African rule, and says that our leaders should emulate their success. Botswana is a tiny country bankrolled by De Beers mining; its governance is generally poor, and failings are masked by easy diamond money.

expertise. Almost all the parts that threaten to drag us down into post-colonial failure are the doing of African prebendalism.

THE VISCERAL APPEAL OF INTEGRATION

Until about halfway through the last century it was normal to be proud of your race. Leaders used *race* and *nation* interchangeably. Germans were racially and nationally *German*; the Italians were also *Italian* both in terms of race and nation, as were Churchill's bulldog *English*. Churchill's historical works trace with pride the rise of *the English race*.

When it comes to race, China today is where pre-WWII Europe was. Over 90 per cent of its 1.4 billion citizens are Han, the world's largest ethnic group. Chinese politicians can discuss race and nation as intertwined concepts.

Why have those of European descent been red-carded from the race-nation game? Three reasons: the Atlantic slave trade, the Holocaust, and the colonial conquest of indigenous peoples. These are the great historical crimes that supposedly confer exceptional moral culpability on Europeans. We were to expunge these sins with integration, opening our race-culture to other race-cultures, proving that colonialism and slavery were aberrations and that our spirit is liberal.

When Martin Luther King marched on Washington in 1963 to give his "I Have a Dream" speech, the world tilted on its axis. Everyone could see dignified people asking only that they be treated fairly. Southern white racists looked stupid and undignified next to civil rights leaders like King, Roy Wilkins, and John Lewis.

It was once my fervent hope that the races would—as King envisaged—happily integrate as free and equal individuals unburdened by racial baggage. When I was a seventeen-year-old student at the University of KwaZulu-Natal in 1987, I showed my commitment to this ideal by joining African students in the *toyi-toyi*, a war dance from the Rhodesian Bush War. By the 1980s, the *toyi-toyi* had become popular in urban protests against the white regime here in South Africa. Regardless of one's political affiliation, the *toyi-toyi* is something of a southern African cultural treasure, an other-worldly expression of African rhythm and song.

When I joined in with the war-dance, it struck me that I had the country all wrong. I had been listening to too much Martin Luther King and reading too much Alan Paton. I had framed South Africa's Struggle as a civil rights movement, a cry for equal treatment within a Western democracy. I had framed it as a struggle for integration. I was not alone in this misreading.

In the 1980s, whites had lost enthusiasm for apartheid, but uhuru was unthinkable. Back then, communism and Africanism were creeds for black radicals. The Chinese, Cubans, and Soviets were the good guys who'd given them arms and succor while Reagan and Thatcher called them *terrorists*. It was an article of faith for leftists that apartheid and capitalism were twin evils.

What the hell was I doing dancing the *toyi-toyi* with a bunch of people who should have been lynching me for living a cushy life of maids and tennis lessons at their expense?

In 1974, I saw Mike Henry in *Tarzan and the Valley of Gold*

(1966). Here was another version of the indigenous-versus-European deathmatch, set in Central Africa. Tarzan is captured by bloodthirsty Africans, who plan to execute him before he is saved in the nick of time by his friends, who kill the tribesmen like so many flies. I sobbed a five-year-old's tears of pity at those poor slaughtered Africans. I truly longed for integration.

Integration has popular appeal. South Africa's greatest team-sport achievement is winning three Rugby World Cups (1995, 2007, and 2019). In 2019, captain Siya Kolisi was one of five Africans in the starting line-up. During the tournament, Mbongi Mbonambi was picked ahead of one of the world's form players, Malcolm Marx. Mbonambi played hooker next to the ex-Zimbabwean "Beast" Mtawarira at prop. Siya Kolisi was one of the flanks, and Lukhanyo Am and Makazole Mapimpi started at centre and left-wing respectively. The other black starter was Cheslin Kolbe, of Cape *coloured* heritage. The bench included Herschel Jantjies, making for a total of seven blacks among the match twenty-three (five Africans including the Zimbabwe-born Mtawarira and two *coloureds*).

The final against England was a dream for the Springboks. I had gathered with a group of friends who had been following the tournament from the start. A few of us shed a tear as Siya Kolisi embraced his mixed-race children on the side of the field after his men had beaten the English 32–12. The *miracle* World Cup Rugby victory of 1995 is redeemed with a truly African success.

Back then, as depicted in Clint Eastwood's film *Invictus* (2009), Mandela convinced his ANC comrades to support the white Afrikaner rugby establishment as an act of faith in the *rainbow nation*.[48] This faith

---

48. There may have been regret on Mandela's part when Louis Luyt, a scion of the Afrikaner rugby establishment, ungraciously dragged President Mandela to court in 1998 over the government's decision to investigate alleged racism in rugby, after which Mandela labelled him a *pitiless dictator*.

in integration was redeemed in 2019. Unlike the 1995 win, Africans weren't bit parts in the white drama, they were central characters. Mbonambi was an inspiration throughout the tournament, the beating heart at the centre of a dominant scrum. The three black backline players created and scored the match-sealing tries. Fans looking for a positive integration story could not have hoped for better.

At the post-match press conference, coach Rassie Erasmus and Siya Kolisi paired up to take questions with the golden Webb Ellis Cup on the table between them. Erasmus shares what they discussed in the build-up to the final: "What is pressure? In South Africa pressure is not having a job; pressure is having one of your close relatives murdered. Rugby shouldn't be something that creates pressure on you, it should be something that creates hope. We started talking about things like: we've got a privilege of giving people hope." Then Erasmus goes on to define what he means by *hope*:

> It's not when you tweet a beautiful tweet—it's when you play a game on a Saturday and people have a nice braaivleis and watch the game and feel good afterwards. And no matter what your political differences or religious differences, for those eighty minutes you agree, whereas on a lot of things you may normally disagree. And that's not our responsibility, it's our privilege to fix those sorts of things.[49]

Towards the end of the press conference, Erasmus is asked to describe the man sitting next to him. He does so by talking about poverty, about not having food to eat, shoes to wear, and a lift to get to school. This is what Kolisi came through, and here he sits savoring a coveted prize of international sport. While Erasmus makes his point he reaches forward and moves the cup a few inches closer to Kolisi's side of the table.

---

49. Transcribed from the original press conference.

Why are our race problems more than a nudge of a trophy away from being resolved? During the press conference, Kolisi starts off thanking and honoring coach Erasmus and his staff. There is mutual respect and genuine affection between the men, as if Erasmus is a father figure to Kolisi.[50]

And yet, the situation is only a clumsy phrase, a slipped racial slur, a political disagreement away from collapsing back into a race war.[51] The Springbok triumph was not depicted as such by everyone. Malema's EFF complained that control of the team was in white hands, which is of a piece with their general point about the country—whites control too much of it. What is the acceptable percentage of African control: 20 per cent? 50 per cent? 100 per cent? Should Rassie Erasmus apologize for being white and for keeping an African out of the top coaching job in the country? Race becomes a fragile issue in South Africa when whites win, especially when the win is depicted as having come at the expense of blacks. Whites are not meant to win at things; they're meant to stand aside for a new group to shine ... but at what cost?

---

50. This is not to suggest that Kolisi is fatherless; his actual father was at the final in Japan.

51. In the wake of George Floyd's killing, a picture off the Internet showed a South African rugby team overseas—which included numerous Springboks—mostly kneeling to honour the call for race equity, but some white players are standing, which many Africans took as a sign of white arrogance.

OUT, DAMNED SPOT!

S tompie James Seipei Moeketsi died on New Year's Eve 1988.[52] Stompie's death is one of several murders attributed to Winnie Mandela and the members of her *Mandela United Football Club* during the crucial years of South Africa's transformation to African rule. Winnie Mandela, who had trained to be a social worker at the Jan Hofmeyr School of Social Work, University of the Witwatersrand, was dubbed by supporters as *the Mother of the Nation*. But journalists Fred Bridgland, Emma Gilbey, and John Carlin present copious evidence that fingers Winnie and her Mandela United Football Club in as many as sixteen murders.[53]

On 11 February 1989, thirteen months after Stompie was killed, Nelson Mandela was released from Victor Verster prison to be warmly embraced by a star, Winnie Mandela. Within those thirteen months, Winnie ordered the murder of Dr Abu Baker Asvat, her personal doctor. Dr Asvat, an anti-apartheid activist, died because he refused to back Winnie's story that the kidnapping of Stompie Seipei (and Stompie's

---

52. The first surname (Seipei) is matrilineal, the second (Moeketsi) is patrilineal.
53. (Gilbey, 1993)

comrades Pelo Mekgwe, Thabiso Mono, and Kenny Kgase) was a rescue operation to save the teens from the homosexual clutches of Methodist priest Paul Verryn.

Asvat examined Stompie on New Year's Eve 1988, telling Winnie, "The boy is seriously ill. He could die at any moment. I cannot save him. You must take him to hospital."[54] That night Stompie was dead; twenty-seven days later Asvat was shot by Cyril Mbatha and Thulani Dlamini. In 1997, Mbatha testified to the Truth and Reconciliation Commission (TRC) that Winnie had ordered the killing, even giving them the murder weapon. Mbatha also told the TRC that the police were not interested in hearing about Winnie's involvement in the crime.[55]

By some interpretations of the story, I have it all wrong: Winnie was not the perpetrator, she was the iconic indigenous victim of a racist white establishment. Was she? Winnie was not entirely indigenous. As biographer Sisonke Msimang notes in *The Resurrection of Winnie Mandela* (2018), Winnie had some European ancestry, inherited via her mother. Besides, her victims were themselves indigenous Africans.

Why didn't the ANC stop her from committing these crimes? They tried—and failed. On being informed about the latest Winnie saga, ANC head Oliver Tambo (exiled in Zambia at the time) lamented, "What must I do? We can't control her. The ANC can't control her. We tried to control her; that's why we formed the Crisis Committee. You must tell the Crisis Committee they must do more."[56] The Mandela Crisis Committee included Struggle luminaries like Beyers Naude, Sidney Mufamadi, Frank Chikane, and Sister Bernard Ncube. With all that moral firepower, they could not save Stompie or Dr Asvat. Bridgland notes that they could have testified against Winnie but, "were more

---

54. (Bridgland, 1997, p. 68)
55. (SAPA, 1997)
56. (Bridgland, 1997, p. 83)

concerned about how the Winnie problem would look to the outside world."[57]

Ordinary Africans were not cowed by the Winnie legend. Her house in Soweto was burnt to the ground by schoolkids retaliating against her thugs.

The white police and justice system were complicit in the conspiracy to shield Winnie. They dismissed the claims of witnesses and did little to protect her victims. The conspiracy to protect Winnie at all costs extended beyond our borders. Although Britain eventually gave refuge to key witness Katiza Cebekhulu, other European countries turned him down for fear of alienating our new elite.[58]

In the interest of a smooth transition from white to black rule, South Africa and the international community made a shameful compromise in dealing with the *Mother of the Nation.*

One of the legends surrounding Stompie Moeketsi was that he memorized the Freedom Charter and quoted from it during political debate. The Freedom Charter was the brainchild of radical white activists. They wanted to canvass black opinion, a courtesy the white supremacist state was vehemently against. In 1955, their idea became reality when the South African Congress Alliance (which included the ANC and its progressive white and Indian allies) sent volunteers to travel the country and ask ordinary Africans about their sociopolitical aspirations.

A segment of African opinion called for the complete removal of whites from the country. But the campaign was organised by a non-racial alliance; such a racial framing was anathema to the project, and so was excluded from the final document. In parts, the Freedom Charter is childlike: "Rent and prices shall be lowered, food plentiful

57. (Bridgland, 1997, p. 83)
58. Cebekhulu was sheltered in Sierra Leone and Equatorial Guinea before moving to more stable conditions in Britain.

and no one shall go hungry." There was also the promise to end laws that controlled the movement of black people, "Fenced locations and ghettoes shall be abolished, and laws which break up families shall be repealed." The document reflects the ideology of well-meaning socialist intellectuals, and an authentic cry for African dignity.

Notwithstanding my cynicism, the Freedom Charter was prescient, anticipating—in some detail—the social democratic values that prevail today. Amazingly, the ANC has delivered on some of those promises. "There shall be a forty-hour work week, a national minimum wage, paid annual leave, sick leave for all workers, and maternity leave on full pay for all working mothers." And, "The aged, the orphans, the disabled and the sick shall be cared for by the state." In 2021, the government was paying welfare grants to at least 12.4 million South Africans.

What exactly did the Freedom Charter mean to Stompie? His effort to memorize it has a ghoulish denouement. Katiza Cebekhulu heard Stompie, in a semi-conscious state, mumbling passages of the document in those last awful hours before Winnie Mandela plunged a dagger through his throat. *A stain that taints us all.*

WHY 'NOTHING HAS CHANGED IN SOUTH AFRICA'

I n her book *What if There Were No Whites in South Africa?* (2015) journalist Ferial Haffajee is perplexed that so many Africans feel that liberation is a chimaera and that the essentially white-supremacist nature of the state has not changed much at all. What?! Our president is African; almost all of our cabinet ministers are African; almost all of the city mayors are African; the heads of the police and military are African; and almost all the heads of other important state institutions, including the Constitutional Court, are African. Should you be in trouble with the law, it is likely that the people who arrest and try you are mostly black. While it's true that many executives in business are white, the boards of major companies are diverse.

The *nothing has changed* position holds that Mandela sold out the African majority and was essentially a puppet for white interests. Which is like the Afrikaner nationalist position that Smuts sold them out to the British. Both are diametrically wrong. In 1989, Oliver Tambo globe-trotted to garner support for the Harare Declaration, the ANC's conditions for entering negotiations with the white government. Tambo had the document signed by all important players, including the Organisation of African Unity (OAU), and it formed the parameters of the deal that ended white rule. The principles of the Harare Declaration were that South Africa should be a united democratic non-racial state. That's exactly what we got.[59]

All the provisos of the Harare Declaration were met in the final agreement that led to the 1994 democratic elections. Any concerns that the white government was not negotiating in good faith should have been dispelled right there. The constitution was signed off by all parties, including radical Africanist parties to the left of the ANC. International commentators could scarcely believe that the National Party had so thoroughly negotiated itself out of power, leaving them with no control over the armed forces, who today report to ANC-appointed generals and ministers. Former DA opposition leader Tony Leon, in his auto-biography *On the Contrary* (2009), claims that Joe Modise, a former ANC bigwig, was bemused that the National Party had handed over the country in exchange for a few cabinet posts.

The constitution makes no provision for a minority veto. Africans make up well more than two-thirds of the country and there is nothing stopping Africans—should enough of them agree—from changing the constitution, within the broad parameters of a rights-based democracy. We are surely living in an *African* state, however you slice and dice the definition.

Haffajee wonders why Africans would consider themselves a minority in South Africa when they constitute over 80 per cent of the population.

South Africa's Struggle took inspiration from America's 1960s Civil Rights Movement. Like some of their sisters and brothers in America, Africans here complain about being *minoritized* by a dominant white culture. In terms of brute political power, this is total

---

59. ANC Struggle hero Albie Sachs made this very same point in a July 2021 interview on South Africans news channel eNCA.

nonsense. Even in terms of commercial power it's a dubious claim. Black Africans have surpassed whites in middle-class consumer spending and heavily outweigh them in overall consumer spending. The great marketing machines that shape opinion and taste are mostly dedicated to meeting *African* aspirations. We are an African-run, African-policed, African-marketed, African-themed country. What's behind the nothing-has-changed story?

I hardly have the courage to write it, but let me try. In South Africa, the dentists, accountants, architects, landscapers, financiers, ecologists, quantity surveyors, entrepreneurs, professional writers, IT professionals, engineers, business consultants, data analysts, commercial farmers, restaurant-owners, corporate leaders, small-business owners, scientists, project leaders, corporate directors, etc. are disproportionately drawn from the minorities: whites, Indians and *coloureds*.[60] These tend to be the people most at odds with the government's vision of the country as a proud African-run state.

Our 1994 transition was welcomed by many from this professional-managerial class; but after Mbeki replaced Mandela and the honeymoon ended, it became increasingly disillusioned with African majority rule.

Our constitution is far from perfect (as discussed in the chapter Our WEIRD Civilization) but there is no doubt that it is suitably designed to encourage the emergence of a professional-managerial class as South Africa's de facto ruling priesthood. In some respects, South Africa has already achieved this. Contrary to the general shortage of professional-managerial skills among our African middle-class, there are many African lawyers. The justices of our Constitutional Court are mainly black African. They can be trusted to follow the directives of

---

60. Of course, there are many Africans too in these roles; but the country depends on minority expertise.

their legal profession; to dignify their hallowed role as high priests of our professional-managerial order.

Alas, that's only part of the story. In the day-to-day running of the country, including the courts, South Africa suffers from grinding venality and lack of direction, the symptom of an incapable state.

It sometimes appears that the officials who are meant to run the country are really serving some other purpose, which is to give credibility to the fiction of indigenous rule. Ironically, radical Africanists like Julius Malema also suspect that this may be the case.

This is the *nothing-has-changed* problem. Those in the professional-managerial class—those who make our modern economy work—are not the same people who won political power in 1994. The professional-managerial class still runs the country and still, by any measure of *race equity*, there are far too few Africans who belong to this class. *Not yet uhuru*, is the complaint of many from our African intelligentsia.

But our ruling elite does not have an indigenous civilization they can draw on to build a viable nation, a civilization to supply them with a professional-managerial cadre to sustain a modern nation.

Africans have not generated the beginnings of a new non-racial civilization here in South Africa. Instead, they have unraveled those pockets of civilization they inherited. The dignity gap has not been closed; the efforts by our elite to *transform* the country into a proud African nation seem only to make things worse.

When our political leaders bemoan *lack of transformation*, it is the crisis of African under-representation at the top table of industry, commerce, finance, and tech to which they refer. But minorities fear that *transformation* has degraded the professions and weakened the business sector. Our thoroughly *transformed* public sector is a shambles.

A news headline reads, "Ramaphosa Decries Lack of

Transformation in Private Sector." The article cites the president's approval of *progress* in the public sector and state-owned entities, where transformation has led to a high percentage of African executives and managers. In the same article, Ramaphosa bemoans the lack of similar levels of transformation in the private sector. Is Ramaphosa aware of the irony? South Africa's state-owned corporations are badly underperforming, costing taxpayers hundreds of billions of rands in bailouts. By contrast, much of our private sector is positively world-class. Without it we become Venezuela, or worse.

Why would the president want to mess with South Africa's private sector when it is saving the country? And why would the president speak proudly of diversity in our dysfunctional public sector?

If South Africa were attracting foreign professionals more than it was losing them, there would be no problem. If foreign investors were turned on by *black empowerment*, *affirmative action*, and the championing of *black industrialists and exporters* (yet another ANC campaign to boost Africans), then transformation would perhaps lead to economic growth. The facts show that foreign investors want a stable state with a merit-based bureaucracy. They don't want to play the indigenous redress game; they simply want to get on with business.

We all know what was *meant* to happen. Africans were *meant* to step into the gap and fill the positions vacated by emigrating minorities. They were *meant* to do what the Afrikaners did and use state power to deliver seismic economic advancement to their people. Africans twice voted to make a president of Jacob Zuma—someone with only an elementary school education and a history of corruption. Testimony from outside and inside the ANC points to the fact that our political elite have signed up for the game of rent-seeking via state access; they're not particularly interested in building a post-industrial bourgeois democracy.

Political scientist Ivor Chipkin notes, "Public servants and officials are the heart of the black middle class, and outside the large metros, provincial government employees, councilors, and local government officials are the black middle class, full stop."[61] The private sector middle-class is overwhelmingly minority races, and they're aggrieved by a state whose main function is not to build a country but to dignify the emerging African elite by giving them jobs and business opportunities.

As Chipkin worryingly observes, "The black [African] middle class has fewer and fewer Diamonds and more and more Grey Suits." In the early years of our non-racial democracy it was the hope that *black diamonds*—emerging black entrepreneurs and professionals—would deracialize our capitalist order and bring dynamism to our economy. The reality is that emerging black wealth often depends on a network of racial regulations more numerous—though not more unjust—than under apartheid. The ANC's welfarist economic policy and its electoral incentive to posture to its African bloc, combine to deliver not a cadre of dynamic black business leaders, but an overly politicized elite who threaten ruin unless they are placated with state-business patronage opportunities. The black bureaucratic class, Chipkin's *grey suits*, bear some resemblance to the *grey shoes*, the Afrikaner bureaucrats of the apartheid era. However, in the latter case the Afrikaners sustained—indeed enhanced—political order and state building.

Today, the grey suits are proving to be a drag on our economy and on state finances, which need a wage cut. According to Chipkin, cutting wages of state employees would be, "effectively, declaring war on the black middle class."[62]

The black middle class is running the country, it's not going to give itself a wage cut. Chipkin bluntly affirms that slashing the government

---

61. (Chipkin, 2020)
62. (Chipkin, 2020)

wage bill, "simply won't happen." The problem with state officials is that, unlike businesspeople and professionals, they're not punished for failure; they won't improve until they face the consequences of their own incompetence. Those who are meant to be the *state-builders* are as likely to be the *state-breakers*, leveraging their majority standing and indigenous credibility to collect rent while race-carding the professional-managerial class into submission.

State Capture is South Africa's most important post-apartheid story. We all agree on what happened, but we're not sure what conclusions to draw. Anton Harber is a left-leaning South African journalist and doyen of his profession. Harber was a fearless critic of the injustices of white supremacy; he continues to uphold his principles in the new South Africa.

His book *So, For the Record* (2020) interrogates how State Capture was covered by the press, exposing how the *Sunday Times*, till recently our most important newspaper, allowed itself to be duped by the gangsters stealing our country. Fortunately, brave journalists from other publications ensured that the *Zuptas*, as the Gupta-Zuma syndicate was nicknamed, received a fair amount of negative press.

In reference to an exposé of the Nkandla scandal, in which President Jacob Zuma illegally used two hundred million rands of state money to refurbish his private residence, Harber writes, "Despite all the state machinery for controlling procurement and tenders, and a constitution that has the highest guarantees of transparency and accountability, it had taken a nosy and intrepid reporter on the ground to spot something odd and ask the right questions, and an editor with an instinct for a good story to publish it."[63]

This is an example of how in the field of journalism a professional from the minorities (Mandy Roussouw) was the constitutional

---

63. (Harber, 2020)

order's last line of defense against tribal politics. Was it only people from the minorities who stood up against Zuma and his criminal gang? No, there were Africans too who were as important in holding the line against him. I've already mentioned Mcebisi Jonas refusing a six-hundred-million-rand Gupta bribe. There was also Public Protector Thuli Madonsela. Although Zuma had appointed her, she showed him no favor in using her office to hold him to account. But even with overwhelming opposition from minorities and from many Africans too, Zuma lasted nine years in office and still no one is in jail for State Capture. Harber describes the ideological coverup of State Capture as follows:

> It was justified in the name of black empowerment. President Zuma and the Guptas were adept at exploiting the ANC's policies to correct the injustices of the past by favoring black businesses and professionals, which in turn favored them. They were taking contracts away from the white-minority owners who'd always dominated industries such as mining, their supporters argued, and they were sharing the opportunities among black people who until recently had been blocked from such enterprises. They were righting historical wrongs, driving the economic transformation that had been so elusive since the political change of 1994.[64]

Sounds like *tribal gangsters repurposing woke thought to steal a country*. That's how I see it but it's not how some Africans see the situation. There was racial hurt at how Indians like Pravin Gordhan were showing them up. When he cleaned up corruption at the South African Revenue Service (SARS), turning it into a world-class organization, there was pushback from some Africans who peddled a narrative that eventually derailed those reforms. According to Harber, "the most

64. (Harber, 2020, p. 117)

insidious and damaging accusation of all" was that "racial discrimination was rife in the organisation, where black African employees were not getting the same treatment and promotion possibilities as others."[65]

The potency of African solidarity was enough to challenge the integrity of our institutions, from journalism to tax collection. However, there was a fightback from the professional-managerial class, one that culminated in a volte-face by the *Sunday Times* in 2016. The paper had stuck to its story of a rogue unit within SARS (led by the singularly scrupulous and efficient Johann van Loggerenberg) that was murderous, racist, and corrupt. When the weight of evidence piled up and broke the credibility of their narrative, they changed editors, submitted an apology, and backtracked. This retreat irked some black journalists.

Piet Rampedi resigned, noting in his resignation letter: "The *Sunday Times* has joined the well-orchestrated media chorus that has abandoned its journalistic ethics in pursuing the narrative that only those who are African are capable of acting illegally, irregularly or in a corrupt manner and those who are Indians and whites aren't, and must be protected at all costs." To which Harber wryly observed: "Since the narrative the paper had carried was one that tore down mostly whites and Indians, this was a strange concern."[66] It was doubly strange given that the new editor who had changed tack on the story, Bongani Siqoko, is himself black African.

Pravin Gordhan and Jacob Zuma are on opposite ends of the ANC's divide around RET (radical economic transformation) and EWC (expropriation without compensation). Zuma is meant to be the transformation radical, yet when he defends himself in court, he often uses white lawyers, while Gordhan consults African lawyers. Zuma plays the race card, while Gordhan is on the defensive for belonging to the wrong race.

---

65. (Harber, 2020)
66. (Harber, 2020)

In November 2019, as minister of public enterprises, Gordhan appointed Andre de Ruyter to head up Eskom. The EFF commented on the appointment, saying among other things, it "reinforce[s] the falsehood that Africans cannot manage strategic complex institutions."[67] I don't remember reading a backlash comment from white business, something like *de Ruyter is a South African citizen who is eligible for the job; the implication that he is not credible and merit-worthy is baseless and defamatory.*

In South Africa, we feel the power of the race card in terms like *radical economic transformation, expropriation of land without compensation, black economic empowerment, white privilege,* and *#rhodesmustfall.* These are indigenous race card slogans. The assumption behind them is: *We black Africans constitute our own civilization and should be allowed to develop that civilization separate from white liberal norms.*

By this calculus, nothing has changed, and nothing ever will change.

---

67. Widely quoted.

SOUTH AFRICA'S RACE WARS

n a critique of Hitler's *Mein Kampf*, George Orwell looks for hidden meaning in the dust-jacket portrait of the author: "It is a pathetic, dog-like face, the face of a man suffering under intolerable wrongs." And: "In a rather more manly way it reproduces the expression of innumerable pictures of Christ crucified, and there is little doubt that that is how Hitler sees himself."[68]

Thabo Mbeki is another politician who has the mien of someone *suffering under intolerable wrongs.*[69] In a 2020 foreword to a book for the South African Democracy Education Trust, he writes: "Barring the 1906 Bambata Rebellion, various late nineteenth century events marked the end of the South African wars of resistance to colonization. They [late nineteenth century events] also saw the emergence of new organisational formations dedicated to the task to secure the rights of the newly oppressed."[70] Mbeki's tortured prose belies a tortured ideology. The ANC has always been confused on the question of whether

---

68. (Orwell, 2017)
69. On the subject, JBM Hertzog *had the air of a man perpetually aggrieved*, according to BK Long in *In Smuts's Camp.*
70. (South African Democracy Education Trust, 2020)

their struggle was about shaking off the chain of colonization, or about securing rights within a Western-based system.

All these years later, Mbeki is still tortured by Africa's weak response to colonial conquest by a small group of Europeans: "The indigenous people engaged in the wars of resistance to colonialism as different communities ... Undoubtedly this contributed to their defeat as the colonizers engaged them sequentially, one after the other." Does Mbeki fantasize about Xhosa, Zulu, Sotho, Pondo, Venda, Ndebele, Tsonga—Khoisan thrown in for good measure—massing as one army in 1880 to drive out the Europeans? Like the Sioux, Apache, Arapaho, Mandan, Navajo, Cherokee, and escaped African American slaves massing in force to drive the white man from the American West?

Mbeki's Africanist religion is a creed of indignity at colonial conquest. It's the hurt that continues to scream its name, the hurt of being on the losing side of a brute race struggle between Africans and Europeans. He cannot acknowledge the truism that Western Civilization had something special to offer Africa. He tells us that African tribesmen resisting colonists was of a piece with Africans in the early twentieth century forming the Ethiopian Church, "to free themselves from control and domination by white Missionaries." Who says? Not all African organizations were dedicated to this narrow creed of anticolonialism. Herein lies a tale about the two-faced ANC, a party that ultimately cares about one thing only: *indigenous rule by any means necessary.*

There's a secret about colonial conquest routinely denied by the anti-racism warriors. Colonial conquest was not so much a struggle between black and white, as a struggle between African tribal polities and the two main white forces, British Imperialism and Boer settler colonialism, both of whom shoved them off their sacred pastoral land, on which tribal order depends.

Over the centuries, ordinary black people have had to artfully shift their loyalties between incompatible ideologies as occasion demanded.

Sometimes (quite often, in fact) their loyalties were with the white man. In a historical echo of our current political contestation, South Africa's colonial wars were not racist battles, with clear lines between the different race-groups. They were mostly battles between African tribesmen against the rest. Our history shows as much. Here are three examples I picked from the litany of South African colonial battles.

1. 1838, 10 April: A second expeditionary force consisting of eighteen [white] Natal traders, thirty Khoi retainers, and some six hundred levies (Zulu servants), four hundred of whom were armed with muskets, crossed the Thukela [river] near its mouth. Seven Zulu regiments, numbering some ten thousand men, under the command of Dingane's brother, Mpande, immediately confronted them, and after a sustained attack, the trader-led group was virtually annihilated.[71]

2. On 7 September 1851, Lieutenant-Colonel Thomas Fordyce, commanding officer of the 74th Highlanders, led a punitive expedition [against the Xhosa] in the Waterkloof made up of 250 regulars, 250 amaMfengu of the Fort Beaufort Levy, and about 150 [white] settlers and Khoikhoi volunteers.[72]

3. In 1834, a Xhosa chief by the name of Maqoma, in revenge for his brother's death, led a raiding army of ten thousand men into the Cape Colony. They … pillaged and burned the homesteads and killed all who resisted. Among the worst sufferers was a colony of freed Khoikhoi who, in 1829, had been settled in the Kat River Valley by the British authorities.[73]

What's going on here? White colonists sought and recruited

---

71. (SAHO, 2022)
72. (Laband, 2020, p. 246)
73. (Wikipedia, 2020)

Africans (often as servants) to help them fight their battles against tribal chiefs. They also sought alliances with Khoisan and with friendly African tribes to overthrow recalcitrant ones. Sol Plaatje, an important chronicler of the injustice of white rule, bemoaned, "It is a standing complaint among educated natives that in South African history books, tribal succor of Europeans is not even as much as mentioned, although tradition abounds with the stories of battle after battle carried by native legions in the cause of European colonization in South Africa."[74] European colonization was achieved with the help of local polities and with the help of Africans who chose to live under European rule rather than indigenous leaders.

However, that's not how our history is depicted by the national culture, as DA parliamentarian Belinda Bozzoli parodies here in her retelling of *the fall*:

> In the myth, good pre-dated evil in the form of the perfect African society, before the fall as it were. In this good African society, there was sufficient land for all, African settlements were spread evenly throughout the land, there were few, if any, Khoi and San people, rulers were benevolent, conflict was minimal, and women and men were equal. Evil came into being in 1652 when white settlers arrived. This initiated the fall. This was, in the myth, followed by a period of nearly three hundred years of unmitigated disaster and conquest. Capitalism and agriculture were the ruthless means through which land was taken, men subjugated, families damaged.[75]

This myth has it that people like Xhosa chief Hintsa (1780–1835) were noble leaders fighting for African rights and dignity against evil whites. Hintsa thought of himself as such, rebuffing attempts by British

---

74. (Willan, 2018, p. 529)
75. (Bozzoli, 2019)

colonial officials to patronize him. On being given a uniform by the British he remarked, "I will wear this when I go to my cattle Kraal and the oxen will come out to look at me."[76] He turned down an invitation from the British colonial government, explaining that "the British colonial governor was not in the habit of visiting other people."[77]

Hintsa was killed by British soldiers in 1835 during the Sixth Frontier War. There were nine Cape Frontier Wars between 1779 and 1879, which were by some accounts, "the longest-running military action in the history of African colonialism."[78]

In a bid to reclaim lost indigenous dignity, Hintsa has been memorialized as a martyr to African freedom. He is honoured by the King Hintsa Bravery Award, which was established in 1999 with the blessing of our government, and is conferred by the Xhosa regent on leaders who emulate the spirit of Hintsa.[79] Jacob Zuma and Robert Mugabe are recipients of the award. That should tell you everything you need to know about race relations in this country. Africans and minorities can all agree that white supremacy was wrong; they will never agree on the Cape Frontier Wars. Since 1994, the ANC government has gone to some lengths to restore the dignity of those like Hintsa and Maqoma who resisted European conquest. They have become heroes in the historical narrative as defending African civilization against foreign onslaught.

The Xhosa lost those nine wars, not because they ran out of arms or warriors, but because they ran out of meaning. Early in the struggle, Xhosa warriors came to understand that European militias were vulnerable to attack in the thick forest during rains when muskets are prone to misfire. But without a rational scientific worldview like the Europeans,

---

76. (Mangcu, 2013, p. 268)
77. (Mangcu, 2013)
78. (Wikipedia, 2020)
79. (Mangcu, 2013)

they could not turn this meaningful tactical discovery into prolonged success. No matter how hard you believe that European bullets will turn to water, as some war-doctors assured their warriors, reality has the last word. As the well-known Philip K. Dick quotation has it, "Reality is that which, when you stop believing in it, doesn't go away."

Ordinary folk did not confront the witchdoctors about their lack of tactical military understanding, they simply melted away to join white society, hybridizing their traditional beliefs with modern ideas. Which is not a whole lot different to what happens today. African elites are unable to build societies that give opportunity to their masses, in which case the aspirant must join foreign societies in search of paid work.

Settler polities—with the opportunity of paid work—became an attractive alternative for tribespeople. By 1848, Xhosa chiefs were not only losing men in battle, they were also losing them to white farmers and to the Cape Colony. Laband tells us that colonial administrator Harry Smith took a census in 1848 that counted only forty thousand amNgqika and amaNdlambe Xhosa. In 1835, there had been over double that number. According to Laband, "most had gone to seek work in the [Cape] Colony."[80] Further, "With migrant labour on this scale, the economic fabric of Xhosa life was in danger of rapidly unravelling." And: "In the past, their resistance to colonialism had been largely about retaining possession of their land. Now, it was also about salvaging what they could of their age-old way of life as it was inexorably engulfed by the advancing colonial order."

What if their age-old way of life was part of the problem? In the late 1850s, the Xhosa fell under the sway of fifteen-year-old prophetess Nongqawuse. According to Laband, she "preached a synthesis of the traditional Xhosa belief in sacrifice for the good of the community and a Christian, mission-trained millennial concept of the apocalypse, of

---

80. (Laband, 2020, p. 227)

the end of days."[81] The Xhosa killed their cattle and burnt their crops because Nongqawuse assured them that this would send Europeans back over the seas. Starvation set in as the Xhosa contributed to their own conquest. Some Europeans looked on with approval, but there was also aid from the colonists.

Intra-African tribal strife meant Europeans could divide Africans to their advantage. In the 1830s, in what is today the North-West Province, the Tswana were repeatedly raided by one of Shaka's ex-lieutenants, Mzilikazi, forcing them into a military alliance with Boer settlers. The 2018 parliamentary hearings into expropriation of land without compensation (EWC) brought dozens of Tswana witnesses to testify how their people had lost ancestral land to the Boers, even if some of that land was traded for help in defending against Mzilikazi.

Some historians claim Mzilikazi's scorched earth control of the Transvaal made it that much easier for the Boers to take ownership of the Highveld. In the late 1830s, the Boers drove out Mzilikazi who ended up founding the Matabele kingdom in southwestern Zimbabwe. That kingdom is no more. Instead, the Matabele (also known as Ndebele) share Zimbabwe with the majority Shona, who dominate the rent-seeking game.

The land once called *Transvaal* has gone through four distinct political orders: Boer Republic (1852–1902); British possession (1902–1910); a province within South Africa's white-run Union (1910–1994); and now a province within an African-dominated state. But still today Boers own the best farmland there. (Except they're not *Boers* anymore, they're members of the professional-managerial class; if forced from their land they can trade their expertise on the international labour market.)

There are similar stories for other parts of the country. In what is today the province of KwaZulu-Natal, after winning the Battle of

---

81. (Laband, 2020, p. 260)

Blood River against the Zulus in 1838, the Boers cunningly exploited two Zulu civil wars (1839 and 1856) to acquire land and cheap labour. Great chunks of that land remain in white hands to this day. But white conquest was achieved with the help of moderate Africans.

The *amaMfengu* (Fengu) fought alongside Europeans against their fellow Africans during those nine Frontier Wars. No-one is quite sure where the Fengu came from. Were they a clan related to the Zulus, fleeing Shaka's expansionist wars in the era known as the *Mfecane* (about 1825)? Or were they disparate Xhosa defectors and migrant laborers for whom the British invented an identity to divide the Xhosa? Even their name was a mystery, mispronounced *Fingo* by Europeans. Plaatje's lament about, "tribal succor of Europeans" is partly a reference to the Fengu. It was a personal matter for Plaatje, given that his wife was one.

The Fengu embodied the promise of European colonialism, that Africans can benefit from Enlightenment values. Here was a different model of dignity to that sought by Hintsa. Here was the Western model of self-improvement through book-learning, Christian values, and loyal service to the British Empire. The Fengu were led by Captain Veldtman Bikitsha (1829–1912), who teamed up with Charles Griffith in leading a force of black and white against the Gcaleka-Xhosa in the Ninth Frontier War (1877), also known as the Fengu-Gcaleka War.[82]

The Fengu started newspapers, built schools, and translated English literature into Xhosa. They were not merely a proxy colonial army; they were indigenous emissaries of European ways. No wonder Plaatje was so bitter at the 1910 betrayal. (More of that in the next chapter.) The spirit of the Fengu was made to look like a carnival act: *clowning Africans imitating European culture.*[83]

---

82. Bikitsha famously said to Queen Victoria, "We have never feared a white man, and we have never lifted our hand against any of your people." They did not fear whites; they emulated them.

83. Plaatje and others did put on *native African acts* for curious European audiences.

The Fengu story takes a surprising turn. Did they become the Uncle Toms of South African history for selling their black brothers down the river? The forerunner to the ANC, the South African Native National Congress (SANNC), was launched in 1912 and was dominated by Gcaleka-Xhosa, whom the Fengu had fought in the Frontier Wars. In the first decade of the organization, Fengu and Gcaleka competed for control in a bitter struggle between those who had sided with the colonial order and those who had resisted it.[84]

But after whites had established the South African Union in 1910, without so much as bothering to consult blacks, and proceeded to take their land and erode their rights, the moderate Fengu position became increasingly untenable. Today, we hear nothing about the betrayal by the Fengu in fighting alongside Boer commandos and British imperialists. We also hear nothing of their decision to adopt European values because they preferred them to tribal ones, and that maybe they had reason to prefer a tolerably decent colonial order to tribal rule.

The betrayal of moderate Africans by white rulers in South Africa is the abiding *iniquity of the fathers*.[85]

---

84. By 1923, when the organization was renamed African National Congress, it was becoming clear that all Africans had become strangers in their own land and that the Union of South Africa was really about the union of whites. The 1923 name change had the desired effect, mostly ending the Xhosa-Fengu squabbles—a happy denouement to an awful period of strife for the amaXhosa.
85. The phrase is from Exodus 20:5.

THE 1910 BETRAYAL

Solomon Tshekisho Plaatje (1876–1932) was an early African Struggle icon who chronicled and criticized the injustices of white domination. He grew up on a German mission station at Doornfontein in the Free State. As a youngster, Plaatje was fascinated by the Israelites of the Old Testament, who seemed so much like his own pastoral people—Barolong Tswana. The Biblical deserts reminded him of the thornveld of South Africa's parched interior, where Plaatje grew up. Here was a story with universal appeal, as Bob Marley and the Rasta movement also believed.

Plaatje had a remarkable talent for music and languages. He was fluent in English, Dutch, and German, and excelled as a clerk of the court within the Cape colonial legal system in Kimberley. In later years he devoted himself to three primary causes: African rights, temperance, and Tswana orthography.

He was widely travelled in the country, well-travelled overseas, and had spent much of his career embedded in the colonial legal system, in which he trusted. He was well-connected to urban and rural black elites; he had the ear of Prime Minister Louis Botha and his deputy, Jan Smuts.

Plaatje was a founding ANC member and the first black South African to write a novel in English, *Mhudi*, written in 1920 and published in 1930. He is also remembered for his book *Native Life in South Africa* (1916), a critique of the 1913 Land Act, for which he interviewed dozens of ordinary Africans whose lives had been destroyed by the act.[86]

In Plaatje, white South Africa had a black leader they could deal with. Here was someone who aspired to Enlightenment ideals, the very ideals Europeans used to justify colonial conquest. A white journalist writing about Plaatje in 1910 in the *Pretoria News* assured his readers, "He is no agitator or firebrand, no stirrer-up of bad feeling between black and white. He accepts the position which the Natives occupy today in the body politic as the natural result of their lack of education and civilization."[87]

Back then, there was a belief among liberal whites that education and civilization, but not race, were justifiable grounds for disenfranchisement. In colonial times, the non-racial Cape franchise was open to all men who owned property worth £75 (or could show an annual income of £50) and who could fill in a registration form in English or Dutch. This policy was psychologically important for Africans. It was, as Plaatje's biographer Brian Willan explained it, the franchise and the legal system, with its "notion of equality before the law" that assured educated Africans of "substance to a vision of a common society in which merit and hard work, and not race, would prevail."[88] This experiment of a multiracial political system proved short-lived and unsupported by Britain.

Britain had vanquished the Boer Republics of the Transvaal and the Orange Free State in the Anglo-Boer War (1899–1902), yet the

86. He literally *got on his bike*, traveling impressive distances to interview them.
87. (Alhadeff, 1976)
88. (Willan, 2018)

blunder of the concentration camps, a blunder that become an atrocity, made it an unpopular war—a Vietnam of its day. Anti-war British voters punished Arthur Balfour's Conservatives in the 1905 election, bringing the Liberal Party's Henry Campbell-Bannerman to power. Liberal Britons could not grasp the nuanced racial scene in South Africa and so gave the governance of the country to the Boers, over the protests of educated Africans like Sol Plaatje.

In 1910—with Britain's blessing—the two colonies (the Cape and Natal) joined with the two ex-Boer Republics (Transvaal and Free State) to form the Union of South Africa. In an echo of the 1885 Berlin Conference, no blacks were part of the agreement to form a South African nation. As Plaatje lamented, "With the formation of the Union, the Imperial Government, for reasons which have never been satisfactorily explained, unreservedly handed over the Natives to the colonists, and these colonists, as a rule, are dominated by the Dutch Republican spirit."[89] (The *Dutch Republican Spirit* was the forerunner to Afrikaner nationalism.)

Poor Plaatje thought of Britain as his people's protector. He could not understand how the Brits, after having recently defeated the Boers, could pass the country back to them over the heads of their erstwhile allies, the Natives. In a sentence, Plaatje sums up the central evil perpetrated by the European race-culture against the African race-culture in South Africa:

> The suzerainty of Great Britain, which under the reign of Her late Majesty Victoria, of blessed memory, was the Natives' only bulwark, has now apparently been withdrawn or relaxed, and the Republicans [Afrikaners], like a lot of bloodhounds long held in the leash, use the free hand given by the Imperial Government not only to guard against a possible superses-

89. (Willan, 2018)

sion of Cape ideals of toleration, but to effectively extend throughout the Union the drastic native policy pursued by the Province which is misnamed "Free" State, and enforce it with the utmost rigor.[90]

For all of Jan Smuts' genius, he never owned up to the evil that would disgrace his legacy. He laid the foundations of white rule in his dealings as a negotiator on the Boer side at the 1902 Treaty of Vereeniging.[91] He convinced the British to leave the matter of black voting rights for the white settlers to decide when they got around to forming Union. When Campbell-Bannerman came to power—eager to right the wrongs of the war—the Boers got their land, plus other lands and other peoples they had no right to rule over.

Disenfranchising blacks was a willful act of white supremacy (it's the very definition of the term) and it set the foundations for harder supremacist attitudes to flourish in the decades to come. In 1906, Smuts wrote: "When I consider the political future of the Natives in South Africa I must say that I look into shadows and darkness; and then I feel inclined to shift the intolerable burden of solving that sphinx problem to the ampler shoulders and stronger brains of the future." Smuts would himself *solve* the problem of a political future for Africans by denying them, as Plaatje explains:

> None of the non-European races in the Provinces of Natal, Transvaal and the "Free" State can exercise the franchise. They have no say in the selection of members for the Union Parliament. That right is only limited to white men, so that a large number of the members of Parliament who voted for this measure have no responsibility towards the black races.[92]

---

90. (Willan, 2018)
91. He was a non-voting member.
92. (Willan, 2018)

His prophecy came to pass when successive white governments (first Hertzog and Smuts in the 1930s and later the apartheid government) whittled away that non-racial Cape franchise to nothing.[93] What was the incentive for white politicians to empower Africans? None. They retained their seats by giving whites ever more privileges at the cost of blacks. As Plaatje lamented: "For to crown all our calamities, South Africa has by law ceased to be the home of any of her native children whose skins are dyed with a pigment that does not conform with the regulation hue."[94]

Could Sol Plaatje have guessed just how celebrated his cause would become? In part thanks to the horrors of Hitler's race nationalism, South Africa became a *cause célèbre*, an issue like no other, uniting even liberals and communists in shared revulsion.

But what was the alternative to white rule in 1910? What vision did moderate Africans like Plaatje, and Xhosa publishing pioneer John Tengo Jabavu have for a multiracial country?[95] Plaatje's biographer Brian Willan explains:

> On the one hand, they [African intellectuals like Plaatje and Jabavu] were faced with constant pressures to reject and disown many of the features of their own societies in order to "prove" their worthiness of entitlement to equal treatment with whites. On the other, they sometimes encountered widespread suspicion on the part of their less educated countrymen for appearing to do precisely this.[96]

Plaatje was eager to bridge black and white cultures; he was a Bob Marley of his day. Like Marley, he was celebrated in Britain and

---

93. Smuts claimed to have done so under sufferance.
94. (Willan, 2018)
95. He founded the country's first Xhosa newspaper.
96. (Willan, 2018)

America, where Plaatje travelled, meeting Marcus Garvey, W.E.B. Du Bois, and other important black figures.

In 1916 (when Plaatje happened to be in England for the tercentenary of Shakespeare's death) the official *Tercentenary Celebration* book included a contribution from Plaatje. He translated six Shakespeare plays into Setswana, two of which have survived for posterity.[97] He rendered William Shakespeare as *Tsikinya-Chaka*, a term he borrowed from a Tswana elder. His friend Alice Werner had watched a Swahili version of *The Merchant of Venice*, commenting, "We now find his works dropping like seed into the virgin soil of the Bantu race," which she believed would enrich "the floating mass of tradition in those wonderful, melodious languages whose future possibilities some of us just dimly apprehend."[98] Plaatje no doubt concurred with the sentiment.

This was the hope of early liberals like Alice Werner, who said, "Shakespeare should be to Africa what Homer and Sophocles were to the European Renaissance."[99] The idea that literature uplifts and edifies predates liberalism and underpins it. Alas, Plaatje's efforts to bring Shakespeare to the people fell afoul of segregationists, who held that Africans should find dignity and meaning within their own cultures and not in European culture. *A hard-right narrative repurposed by the hard-left today.*

Why was Plaatje so interested in Shakespeare? Willan explains:

> he admired Shakespeare precisely because he found in him a
> humanity that transcended boundaries of race and colour in a
> way that so many later English writers conspicuously failed to

---

97. According to Willan, his translation of *Comedy of Errors* was published in his lifetime, while his translation of *Julius Caesar* was published posthumously. His translations of *Othello, Romeo and Juliet, The Merchant of Venice*, and *Much Ado About Nothing*—but for a few surviving pages—are lost to history.
98. (Willan, 2018, p. 399)
99. (Willan, 2018, p. 300) Werner being quoted by Willan; I've rearranged the words slightly but have retained the meaning.

do; he thought many of the themes with which Shakespeare was concerned ... had a direct impact with their [Tswana people's] own history and traditions; and in the act of translation, he sought not to reproduce directly the poetic qualities of Shakespeare's language, but to match them, to find equivalents in Setswana, to demonstrate its own wealth of expression.[100]

Plaatje translated Shakespearian idioms into Setswana and Setswana idioms into English; his *Sechuana Proverbs* (1916) has 1,132 sayings, idioms, and short tales in the original Tswana with their English equivalents. [101]

Despite his love of African languages, Plaatje would perhaps have agreed with the African journalist writing for the newspaper *Imvo Zabantsundu* (Black Opinion) in 1895:

The key of knowledge is the English language. Without such a mastery of it as will give the scholar a taste for reading, the great English literature is a sealed book, and he remains one of the uneducated, living in the miserably small world of Boer ideals, or those of the untaught Natives. But besides, in this country where the English are the rulers, the merchants, and the influential men, he can never obtain a position in life of any importance without a command of English.[102]

Here is the standard pre-1960s approach to integration: educated Africans, by learning its language and ways, should be allowed to join Western culture and enjoy its privileges.

Why did things change? Unfortunately, back in 1895, Europeans were generally racist, unwilling to open their societies to blacks,

---

100.(Willan, 2018, p. 503)
101. According to Willan, the first edition of the book had 732 proverbs, with the second edition adding another 400.
102. (Willan, 2018, p. 36)

regardless of whether they embraced European values or mastered European culture. In South Africa this racist approach stayed institutionalized for a century on from 1895, condemning Africans to a one-hundred-year wait to be treated as equal citizens in the land of their forefathers.

The early ANC moderates valued Christianity and embraced literature and law to dignify their struggle, to show they were not against Europeans or against European civilization. On the contrary, they felt themselves to be the very conscience of that civilization.

Josiah Gumede, Saul Msane, Pixley ka Seme, Sol Plaatje, and Tengo Jabavu were intellectuals who exhorted whites to open the gates of civilization to deserving Africans ... such as themselves. Back when the ANC was formed in 1912, they would have accepted political rights based on colour-blind tests of citizenship. They referred to themselves as *civilized* and complained that many of their fellow *natives* (or *savages*) lived in a state of *barbarism*. Their thinking betrayed some support for the prevailing European idea that it alone stood at the apex of cultural evolution.

When the ANC met in March 1918 for its sixth annual conference, there was a split: radicals from the Transvaal (the country's mining-industrial crucible) versus moderates from the other three provinces (Cape, Orange Free State and Natal).[103] The Transvaal delegates represented urban Africans fighting for workers' rights. These workers had experienced the power of industrial action and had been exposed to communist thinking. Sol Plaatje, in a letter to De Beers, parodied their socialist fervor: "The ten Transvaal delegates came to Congress with a concord and determination that was perfectly astounding and foreign to our customary native demeanour at conferences. They spoke almost in unison, in short sentences, nearly every one of which began and ended

---

103. This was when it was still called the SANNC.

with the word 'strike'."[104]

The history of the ANC shows a tension between the radicals (those fighting for their African race-culture against the European one) and the moderates (those seeking equal rights for Africans within the dominant European race-culture). The white response to this African political aspiration came in three flavors: 1. Racist: using our European race-culture to dominate the African race-culture; 2: Marxist: using the African race-culture to defeat the unjust class structure inherent in the European race-culture; and 3. Liberal: including Africans in our European race-culture.

Since the nineteenth century in South Africa, white liberals and African moderates agreed that Africans should join the European race-culture on mostly colour-blind terms. Today, this position is considered old-fashioned and possibly even racist for perpetuating the legacy of white cultural dominance. But we either form a country based on standard liberal values, or we revert to race nationalism.

It turns out that the *standard liberal values* many of us agree on tend to be part of the European race-culture heritage. I unapologetically hold up my own race-culture as being worthy and worth defending. I also hold it up as the world's finest example of integration. As someone who identifies as part of this race-culture, I think I speak for many when I say I don't want to be exclusionary and racist, yet I want to retain coherence and continuity of my race-culture. I am happy for the victories of multiracialism over sectarianism, but I don't want to compromise the values of my civilization for the sake of race equity. I don't believe in bringing one race down to help another race.[105] I don't believe that the answer to hate is more hate.

---

104. (Willan, 2018, p. 339).
105. Which is what many have tried to do to the Ashkenazi Jews, the world's leading Nobel Prize-winning race-culture.

PATON'S MIRACLE OF *AGAPE*

O n 1 February 1948, publishers Charles Scribner's Sons, based in New York City, released a book by a first-time author from South Africa called Alan Paton. *Cry, the Beloved Country* went on to sell millions of copies in America and across the world, and is compared to Harper Lee's *To Kill a Mockingbird* (1960) for helping nudge the culture toward racial tolerance.

There are two film adaptations of *Cry, the Beloved Country*. The latter one (1995) starred Richard Harris and a woefully miscast James Earl Jones. The book was also turned into a musical, *Lost in the Stars* (1949), with a music score by Kurt Weill and script by Maxwell Anderson. Charles Scribner's Sons have published the book six times, most recently in 2003.

The novel is about a sixty-year-old rural Natal priest, Stephen Kumalo, who makes his maiden trip to Johannesburg to find his relatives who have left the village for the opportunities of the big city. One of those relatives is his son Absalom. Kumalo arrives in Johannesburg too late to save Absalom, who faces trial for murder; the result of an armed robbery in which Absalom is involved.

Paton's novel pushes two serious buttons: black-on-white crime, and the incompatibility of African culture with city living. The book is not a political novel; it's an exploration of the power—and limits—of Paton's Christian faith. The narrative creates a cauldron of impossibly difficult race-culture conundrums, testing the faith and dignity of its characters. Reverend Stephen Kumalo's dignity remains intact, but his urbanized brother John Kumalo is corrupted by money, power, and the easy pleasures of city living.

Who was Alan Paton to lecture us about race and Christian faith?

Paton started his career as a math teacher in Natal to white pupils. In 1935, he successfully applied to head up Diepkloof Reformatory (for African juvenile delinquents).[106] From 1935 to 1948, Alan Paton was the most important male figure to thousands of neglected African boys. He was driven by a zeal to give these boys a redeeming human touch—some love in a lonely world. Paton was inspired by *agape*: Christian love. He believed that Christian love had the power not only to reform delinquents but to heal the country's racial strife.

Did Alan Paton successfully *agape* his African boys from the moral wasteland of crime to the warm embrace of civilization? Yes! Diepkloof's rates of absconding and recidivism compared favourably to the best reformatories of the day.[107] Paton's system of tough love and rewarding good behaviour with greater freedom worked wonders. Well over 90 per cent of the boys responded by spurning crime and becoming responsible citizens.

James Gebevu, an African teacher at Diepkloof, once accused Paton of being racist.[108] After looking "deep into my heart," as he put it, Paton didn't like what he saw and apologized to Gebevu, planting a tree on the reformatory grounds as an act of racial reconciliation.

106. The reformatory would have included African and *coloured* boys.
107. See Alexander's biography for the full details on this. (Alexander, 1994)
108. (Alexander, 1994)

Gebevu forgave him. When the Afrikaner nationalists came to power in 1948, the Afrikaner staff at Diepkloof made it their duty to eat separately from the African staff, even doing so at Paton's farewell party. This brought him to tears of grief.

Paton had friends and associates of all colors and never condescended to a black person by putting on a pidgin accent or speaking *Fanakalo*.[109] He treated employees with respect, resisting the protestations of his wife in letting his factotum, Sikali, enjoy cannabis-fueled parties on his property.

Paton was something of a self-publicist, not above playing the political game to trumpet his achievements and fight for more resources to continue his good works. Reports of his success at Diepkloof appeared often enough in the press. Helped by his superb writing, he was making a potent counterclaim against the ideology of white supremacy. He proved that African delinquents could, with love and discipline, be taught to operate within the constraints of civilization.

This success of Christian *agape* love, bounded within institutional discipline, came to the attention of a man more rooted in Old Testament thinking—Hendrik Verwoerd, editor of the Afrikaner nationalist newspaper *Die Transvaler*. The paper was anti-Smuts, anti-black, and anti-South Africa's support of Britain against Nazi Germany. In a May 1945 editorial Verwoerd wrote, "Diepkloof as an institution to reform young black delinquents [is] a colossal failure." He mocked Paton's *mollycoddling* theories and complained about chronic *abscondment* and the *loafing* about the farm of black *ladies and gentlemen*, to whom the white staff had been ordered to say *asseblief tog* (kindly please) to get them to do anything.[110] Never mind that Verwoerd's claims were untrue, they made for powerful propaganda in a time of rising Afrikaner nationalist feelings.

---

109. This is a pidgin tongue used on South Africa's mines.
110. (Alexander, 1994)

At Diepkloof Reformatory, Alan Paton taught black boys how to dignify their lives. He was a Christian hero of his time. In attacking Paton, Hendrik Verwoerd acted in bad faith, twisting words and distorting meaning to fulfil a sectarian agenda ... or not.

Maybe Verwoerd had to harden his heart to the *little black gentlemen* of Diepkloof Reformatory because there was no other way to safeguard the future of his race-culture. If that is the case, then it's unfortunate that Verwoerd was not only mean-spirited about Paton's *little black gentlemen*, but he was also mean-spirited about investing in his own vision for the country.

In 1954, Verwoerd, as minister of native affairs, was advised by the Tomlinson Commission (appointed by government) that he should throw at least 100 million South African pounds at the Bantustans if he wanted his policy of separate development to work. Verwoerd was not prepared to go any higher than 36.6 million pounds and so the scheme was doomed before it had even started.[111]

In 1948, Paton was on the wrong side of South African history. As mentioned previously, South Africa's voting system back then was almost exclusively for the white population, of which Afrikaners made up 60%. Add to that the fact that rural constituencies could be constituted with 15 per cent fewer voters than urban ones. (Afrikaners were more rural than English-speaking South Africans.) Thanks to this skewed electoral system, in 1948, the country fell under the sway of a vengeful sectarian agenda: Afrikaner nationalism.[112] The electoral system gave the country to whoever could inflame the political passions of the most racist segment of South African society.

---

111. These figures are from Wikipedia; it's common cause that the apartheid government did not follow the full recommendations of the report, but instead skimped on it.
112. Verwoerd heaped further indignity on Paton when in 1950, as minister of native affairs, he set about closing Diepkloof Reformatory.

That party was the Herenigde Nasionale Party (Reunited National Party), later to return to its original name, Nasionale Party (National Party). Their galvanizing cause was Afrikaner nationalism, the idea that the country belonged to white Afrikaners, who had a special destiny to rule over other races, and who owed no loyalty to Britain.

The party was formed in 1939, in response to a parliamentary vote on South Africa's involvement in the Second World War. The deputy prime minister, Jan Smuts, wanted South Africa to join Britain in its war on Nazi Germany; Prime Minister JBM Hertzog favored neutrality. Smuts, who enjoyed support from English-speaking parliamentarians, as well as moderate Afrikaners, narrowly won the parliamentary vote on the war, taking over as prime minister and committing men and national resources to the cause … once again.

In 1914 he had done so as minister of defence, now he was doing so as prime minister. Hertzog and his supporters joined with DF Malan's Gesuiwerde Nasionale Party (Purified National Party), to form the Herenigde Nasionale Party. Hertzog was given leadership of the party, which he lost to Malan in due course because of his moderate views on the *race question*. (The term back then described relations between Afrikaners and English-speakers.) DF Malan wanted Afrikaners to retain their cultural distinctiveness from the English, an ideology that Hertzog had little passion for, which made him unpopular among the Nationalist base.

Malan was a cleric and theologian in the Dutch Reformed Church, at the time an all-white church for Afrikaner protestants. His name appears in an anecdote about the British entertainer George Formby, who boosted troop morale during the Second World War with his naughty ditties, played on his ukulele and sung in a high-pitched Lancashire accent. Formby's biographer David Bret tells of Formby performing in South Africa in 1946, two years before Malan became prime minister. After a show for a black crowd, a young black girl presented gifts to the performers, at which point she was embraced by Formby. When Malan telephoned Formby to complain, his wife/manager Beryl Ingham answered the call, responding with: "Why don't you piss off, you horrible little man?"[113]

Malan formed his *Purified* National Party in 1935 out of disgust at the sociopolitical merging of Afrikaner and English. He wanted to keep the Afrikaners pure and separate, politically distinct from the culturally confident English. He wanted to use political office to create an Afrikaner identity.

At the expense of a sustainable political order for South Africa, his National Party achieved its goal of boosting Afrikaners to the socioeconomic level of English-speaking whites. By the 1970s Afrikaners finally joined the world's other white protestants in elevating themselves to middle-class status. Upward mobility liberalized the Afrikaner establishment; as soon as the Afrikaners became bourgeois, Afrikaner nationalism started disappearing like snow in the rain.

By the 1980s, the National Party had become as popular—if not more so—with English-speaking whites as it was with Afrikaners, many of whom opposed President PW Botha's modest reforms. These right-wing Afrikaners, the dying vestiges of white supremacy, voted for Andries Treurnicht's Conservative Party, which promised white voters a return to strict apartheid. Treurnicht was nicknamed *Dr No* for resisting Botha's reform agenda.

In 1984, my high school hosted Treurnicht for a debate. At my private English-speaking school plenty of our teachers and pupils were sufficiently liberal to feel a visceral disgust at Dr No's hardline views. During question time, a liberal Christian stood up from the audience, Bible in hand, defying Treurnicht to find God's backing for his odious ideas.

---

113. (Louvish, 2002)

Treurnicht, who had been a minister in the Dutch Reformed Church for fourteen years, handled the questions remarkably well. We all knew how wrong he was, but we couldn't pin him down and make him suffer. That's until our headmaster Neil Jardine asked a question from the chair: "In light of the inclusion of black players and black teams at the interprovincial schools rugby tournament and noting that nothing untoward or undignified came of the new ruling in favor of multiracial sports, can you please explain why we should revert to seg-regated sports?"[114] Finally, Dr No was stumped.

If the Afrikaner nationalists had adopted a more nuanced idea about race, they could have gotten away with their supremacy for a bit longer. Instead, they turned on the very people who could confer their rule credibility, the *coloureds*, many of whom spoke their language and shared their cultural heritage, as well as a fair chunk of their genetic heritage. This was not sane politics, but revenge for the concentration camps, where the British had enjoined African and *coloured* to do some of their dirty work.

The events of 26 May 1948, when DF Malan unexpectedly found himself prime minister, changed Paton's life, which had already been turned upside down with the immediate success of *Cry, the Beloved Country*. Pollution and purity are important political forces, especially on race, where genetic codes nudge us towards fear of one another. Paton's stories invite the reader to replace racial fear with love.

The timing of *Cry*—coeval with apartheid—was a portent worthy of Paton's epic plots. The novel starts with that famous Biblical lilt: "There is a lovely road that runs from Ixopo into the hills. These hills are grass-covered and rolling, and they are lovely beyond any singing of it." He roots this Biblical lilt in the soil: "Stand unshod upon it, for the ground is holy, being even as it came from the Creator. Keep

---

114. The tournament is called Craven Week.

it, guard it, care for it, for it keeps men, guards men, cares for men. Destroy it, and man is destroyed."

Alan Paton was a keen birdwatcher, his notations on South Africa's impressively diverse bird population was a prized possession. He appreciated diversity in nature and in humanity … unlike DF Malan.

The 1951 film adaptation *Cry, the Beloved Country* starred two great African-origin actors of the era, Canada Lee and Sidney Poitier. Zoltan Korda directed. The Wikipedia entry for the film tells us that:

> Since the country was then under apartheid … stars Sidney Poitier and Canada Lee and producer/director Korda devised a scheme where they told the South African immigration authorities that Poitier and Lee were not actors but were Korda's indentured servants; otherwise, the two black actors and the white director could have been arrested, and jailed without trial.

The source for this claim is uncited; that's because it's only partly true. In a metaphorical sense, Poitier and Lee had to justify their presence in the country by being part of a white project. Would the newly minted apartheid government really throw these world celebrities into prison for being black? *No!* But it's true that Poitier and Lee were greatly affected by the racism they saw around them.

South African film historian and archivist Thorsten Wedekind writes that Poitier's experience of racism in South Africa, "invoked vivid & unpleasant memories of being the frequent victim of racism as a teenager in Miami. It created a deep-rooted & lasting impression that remained with him throughout the years as he became a major star, and was, no doubt, one of the motivations in accepting the role in the anti-apartheid thriller *The Wilby Conspiracy* (1974)."[115]

---

115. From Thorsten Wedekind's manuscript for the index of South African films.

Dr DF Malan and his wife, Mrs Maria Malan, attended the gala opening of *Cry, the Beloved Country* in Johannesburg in early 1952. Commenting on the film's depiction of the urban squalor that blighted African life, Mrs Malan asked Paton, "Do you really think that Joburg looks like that?"[116]

In 1953 Paton helped to form the Liberal Party of South Africa, serving as its founding co-vice-president and then president till its dissolution in 1968; a forced move after the apartheid state banned political organization across the color line.

Like Malan, Paton was a committed Christian. However, Paton's views about sanctity, pollution, and degradation were different from Malan's. Not for Paton the negro-phobia and Calvinist suppression of Afrikaner nationalism. Not for him the base white politics of the *would-you-want-your-daughter-to-sleep-with-a-black-man?* variety.

Paton writes in some detail about his successes and failings in matters of love and romance. He wrote approvingly of sex, dealing with the subject in a spirit of sacred sensitivity. Paton was a man of formidable energy and drive. He was also a family man who loved his wife, Dorrie, returning to her after straying once or twice.

In her autobiography, *Some Sort of a Job* (1992), Anne Hopkins—whom Paton married after Dorrie's passing—writes of being bemused at Paton's angry outburst at finding his stepdaughter canoodling with a boyfriend.[117] His repressed Christadelphian upbringing possibly expressed itself as a mixture of prudishness and prurience.[118]

Is it fair to talk about a shadow aspect of his character? Paton was not kindly remembered by *all* of his pupils. Some of his former students at Ixopo High School and Maritzburg College, interviewed by Paton's biographer in the 1990s, were still bitter at his beatings. His

116. Paton tells the story in his autobiography *Beyond the Mountain*.
117. (Hopkins, 1992)
118. A Christian sect that follows different beliefs than mainstream denominations.

notebook shows that he administered beatings regularly and often at Diepkloof.[119]

As a young teacher at Ixopo, he admitted to having fallen in love with one of his students, the daughter of a local farmer, and joked about the possibility of the enraged father coming after him with a shotgun. He never acted on his desire for the girl, instead directing his deep longings towards Dorrie Lusted, a married woman a few years his senior. Dorrie's husband was terminally ill; when he died the two conducted their affair with the tact and sensitivity that circumstance demanded. A few years into the marriage, Paton became enamored with a young woman from the local tennis club. After a brief fling, he confessed. When his wife asked what he was going to do about his infatuation, Paton replied, "End it."

After Dorrie died in 1967, Paton seems to have enjoyed a patch of freedom. He was sixty-four years old and fortunate to have money, fame, a circle of supportive friends and good health. If he had found marriage to be sexually constraining at times, here was a chance to let loose. It was, after all, the late 1960s. On 6 March 1968, driving home after dinner and drinks with close friends, he stopped for a hitchhiker by the name of Derek Ndhlovu. Paton made a habit of giving rides to black people, taking the opportunity to canvass their opinion on issues of the day.

What happened after he stopped to give Ndhlovu a lift was the subject of conjecture at a trial on 25 July that year, in which Ndhlovu claimed that Paton had asked him to procure the sexual services of a woman. Ndhlovu testified that he had procured a certain Alice Ngcobo who agreed to "have an affair with Paton in the car or on the grass" where they stood, which was Clermont township, just inland of

---

119. Facts are taken from Peter Alexander's biography of Paton.

Durban.[120] When Paton said he'd prefer to take her back to his home, Ndhlovu feared he would lose out on his agreed-upon R10 fee. And so Ndhlovu assaulted Paton and robbed him of R31.60, plus his watch and coat. In the melee, Paton managed to press the hooter which alerted a nearby resident, off-duty security policeman Alfred Khumalo ... *that name*. Khumalo (who later brought the matter to trial) immediately recognised Paton, having once tailed him as part of his police duties.[121]

At the trial, all four characters gave somewhat contradictory accounts, with pimp and prostitute—Ndhlovu and Ngcobo—closest in detail. Judge FJ Dietzsch gave Ndhlovu two years of "corrective training" for robbery, and exonerated Paton and Alice Ngcobo; but Dietzsch did not rule out the possibility that Paton had tried to procure her services.

Peter Alexander connects this incident to the mysterious death of Paton's father, James, a "tormented personality."[122] In May 1930, James Paton had gone on one of his customary long hikes into the hills, never to return. Alexander suggests, with some circumstantial justification, that James Paton's obsessive discipline and protectiveness over his daughters' virtue masked an uncontrolled libido; and that his long walks included forays into African villages in search of easy sex. James Paton's decomposed body was found face-down in a stream a month after he'd set out on his walk. He was perhaps strangled by Africans, intent on robbing him, or in vengeance for abusing their daughters.

Alice Ngcobo questioned Paton at the trial, asking if he had also given a lift to a woman. Paton denied this, at which she asked, "Then how do I come into the picture?" To which Paton replied: "I don't

---

120. (Alexander, 1994, p. 353)
121. Paton's biographer Peter Alexander reveals evidence that Paton later paid for the education of Khumalo's children.
122. Ibid (p. 4)

know."[123] After the charges were cleared Paton threw a party in celebration, at which his sons wryly commented to each other about how unrepentant he was after his legal escape.

Paton had been saved by Alfred Khumalo, the type of person he had written about and a near namesake to his famous fictional character Stephen Kumalo from *Cry, the Beloved Country*. I was about eleven when I read that book, and I cried like I did when I saw Tarzan and his friends slaughtering Africans. Were they the same tears? By eleven I had developed something of a political conscience. Thanks to an obsession with Bob Marley's *Rastaman Vibration* album (1976), I had an appreciation for diversity. Alan Paton did his best to dignify the lives of Africans. For style and metaphor he turned to the Bible; it didn't always work, but it worked well enough to conscientize millions across the world about the evils of white supremacy. (Which is more-or-less what you can say for Bob Marley.)

But Paton was at odds with the central force that overturned white rule: African urban migrancy. Radical black activists never quite forgave him for writing *Cry,* in which urban migrancy is depicted as degrading for Africans, robbing them of their traditions and values. No matter his political commitment to liberalism, Paton's literary imagination led him to a place not that different from the white supremacists—implying that Africans develop in a different way from what we do, and that the shock of Westernization and urbanisation is not necessarily good for them.

In Johnny Clegg's song "Third World Child" he sings: *You should learn to speak a little bit of English, Don't be scared of a suit and tie, Learn to walk in the dreams of the foreigner, I am a third world child.* This is the *Jim Comes to Joburg* trope.[124] Jim is the rural African who

---

123. Ibid (p. 353)
124. This is the title of a 1949 South African film, from which the term originates.

migrates to Gauteng, the country's great mining-industrial crucible. According to the song, the African migrant worker must cross a *no-man's land* to find his *stolen jewel*.

The apartheid government wanted to keep Africans in rural areas and out of urban ones. But many Africans had been dispossessed of their farmland, and so were forced into urban migrancy, where mines and factories absorbed them as cheap labour. Economic expediency trumped the apartheid ideal of keeping Africans out of cities. The effect on Africans was momentous. As John Matisonn notes, "The unholy coincidence of political pressure with the interests of business in cheap, docile labour combined to cripple, for a long time, the cultural and political expression of a people."[125] This was the stolen jewel that Africans needed to retrieve.

African political expression did eventually come to the fore in urban centres as migrants increasingly settled there. Here they mixed with Africans from all parts of the country, replacing ties of kin and tribe with universal ideals, and forging a shared consciousness. The African unity that the ANC had been preaching since 1912 was made reality by a brutal system of land confiscation and labour exploitation.

From the 1950s, in towns and cities, Africans fought for their dignity through politics, culture, and business. No matter where they came from or what African language they spoke, in an urban setting they could easily identify their class enemy. Urbanized working-class and middle-class Africans are key to understanding South Africa's sociopolitical dynamics. Apartheid's stiffest battles were against trade unions, churches, schools, colleges, universities—the institutions of modern civilized society. It was mass black urbanization that ulti-mately defeated white rule. Decades of economic expediency by white supremacists finally came back to haunt them.

---

125. (Mattison, 2015, p. 48)

BIKO'S SEGREGATION

In his novella *Mrs. Plum* (1967), the well-known South African writer Es'kia Mpahlele depicts a white Johannesburg liberal from the perspective of her African cook, Karabo. Mrs Plum's anti-apartheid activism and her seemingly liberal attitude to race are at odds with her instinctive sense of white superiority. Mpahlele mercilessly satirizes her for not being who she pretends to be.[126] When things become more real and a black man wants to sleep with her daughter, Mrs Plum fails the test. She encourages the daughter to break off her affair with the African doctor on the grounds that ... well, on no grounds at all other than race.

Mpahlele's story is about Karabo's growing political consciousness in a country where—as a rule—the employers were white and the domestic workers African. Notwithstanding Mrs Plum's efforts to expand Karabo's horizons by giving her reading material and inviting her to share meals, Karabo still identifies strongly as African, finding friendship and shared experience at the Black Crow Club, a support

---

126. Mpahlele stretches the bounds of decency by having Karabo witness Mrs. Plum in a scene bordering on bestiality.

group for domestic workers. Karabo is most at ease among people who share her background. The story is a sobering assessment of the limits of integration: whites are exposed as hypocritical racists, and the African protagonist develops a segregationist identity.[127]

Mpahlele's interpretation of white attitudes was emblematic of the era's stirrings in race relations. Blacks had become tired of reaching out to whites only to be rebuffed or patronized. Seeking integration with whites comes at a cost, like the pain in Karabo's heart at having the African doctor prefer a white woman to her.

Bantu Stephen Biko (1946–1977) came of age during this new era of race relations. As a student leader, he rejected non-racialism in favor of black consciousness. Steve Biko was behind the 1968 formation of the South African Student Organisation (SASO) to split black students away from the multiracial liberal body NUSAS.[128] Even though SASO was banned and eventually superseded by the ANC-aligned COSAS, Biko's black consciousness ideas prevailed. By the time I was studying at the University of Natal (1987–1990), COSAS was exclusively for blacks and NUSAS for whites. Both preached *non-racialism*—a confusing term. Non-racialism meant all sorts of things except for what you may expect it to mean. The guiding principle of the anti-apartheid non-racial alliance was that whites and Indians could join in and collaborate with them, but Africans should lead the Struggle against white supremacy, and be seen to be doing so.

Non-racialism has proven to be the ultimate bait-and-switch strategy. It promised to fix our racial woes by nixing them: *Let's put a non in front of race but still insist on African leadership.* Today, we rue our support for non-racialism, which has delivered a venal African order. Biko was at least more honest. His organization's (SASO) 1971

---

127. Interestingly, Mpahlele considers *Mrs. Plum* one of his best works.
128. He started studying medicine before changing to law a few years in.

manifesto defined blacks as those "who are part of the solution" and whites as those "who are part of the problem."[129]

Was Biko anti-white? Not in his personal affairs. He enjoyed friendships with white men and women, including the odd romantic liaison with the latter. But he was a segregationist of sorts. He felt that whites undermined blacks in political organizations by being bossy and by assuming initiative and leadership for themselves.

Biko was interested in blacks first finding each other and then meeting whites as a united front dedicated to black pride and indigenous redress. Biko could—to paraphrase Kipling—*talk with crowds and keep his virtue, walk with Kings and not lose the common touch.* What got Biko interested in politics was not ideas about equality, but an unjust beating from white policemen like those who murdered him in September 1977.

Biko was a race nationalist who was unconvinced by liberal white attempts at integration. He reasoned that it's impossible for whites to fix the country's core race problem: a black pride deficit. Why were his black consciousness organizations (SASO and the Black People's Convention) superseded by the *non-racial* ANC and its Congress movement allies? One reason is that the Congress movement drew on the skills and initiative of whites, including a small group of highly influential Jewish communists.

Biko was rightfully concerned about this approach. Whites had completely different reasons than Africans for opposing white supremacy. Whites were motivated by humanist idealism, while Africans were motivated by a desire to redeem their defeated civilization, avenge the ancestral hurt of colonial domination, and eventually cash in on the political dividend of championing the majority cause. While fighting a common enemy—the white supremacist state—differences could be

129. (South African History Online, 2019)

papered over; but since 1994, the white, Indian, and *coloured* radicals from the minorities have also become disillusioned with the direction of the country.

Including whites and Indians in their movement was a tactical decision by the ANC. They believed they could benefit from the well-meaning energy and intelligence of these folks without compromising their Africanist values. There is a fine line between a tactical decision and an expedient one. Sol Plaatje was aware of the conundrum and warned against, "leaving white people to fight our battle for equal treatment and equal recognition."[130]

Did those liberal white students heed Biko's advice to get out of black politics? Not at all. Perhaps eager to prove their radicalism, they transitioned from Alan Paton's liberalism to Marxism, which they preached to African workers.[131] This was not Biko's idea of race relations. As his friend Barney Pityana put it, "The main thing was to get black people to articulate their struggle and reject the white liberal establishment from prescribing to people."[132]

After inspiring the launch of the Black People's Convention, Biko tried to organize a front of black consciousness organizations inside the country. This was in the wake of the Soweto Uprising that had begun on 16 June 1976 and the independence victories in Mozambique and Angola a year before that. In September 1977, Biko travelled from King William's Town in the Eastern Cape to Cape Town to meet Neville Alexander, leader of a radical black consciousness organization. (Alexander was *coloured.*) For some reason, Alexander's party had decided that he "should not meet Biko at that time". As Alexander later explained, "I had not been mandated to see him and could not get a mandate in time."

---

130. (Willan, 2018, p. 453)
131. (Mattison, 2015)
132. (South African History Online, 2019)

Biko was driven around Cape Town to find Alexander. Then when they found him, Biko waited three hours while interlocuters fruitlessly pleaded his cause. In later years, Alexander confessed, "He stood two metres away from my backdoor and I refused to meet him, as much as I would have liked to have done so." For three hours, Biko waited in the car, and for three hours, Alexander stood firm … to his deep regret: "When I look back I realise that this is perhaps the folly of being too principled. I was so hard, I was so principled … I am really sorry that the meeting never happened."[133]

A bitterly disappointed Biko, with his comrade Peter Cyril Jones at the wheel, headed back to King William's Town, only to be intercepted at a police roadblock near Grahamstown—the ultimate frontier town.[134] Both Biko and Jones were arrested. Biko spent weeks in detention before dying of brain hemorrhaging caused by blows to the head. It was not a political assassination so much as an act of white supremacist hate. One that sparked a global backlash against the apartheid regime.

At a National Party meeting shortly after Biko's death, minister of justice Jimmy Kruger stated, to applause and laughter, "The death of Biko leaves me cold." The liberal media portrayed Kruger as a pinup apartheid hate figure, a short brutish common Afrikaner.[135] Prime Minister John Vorster was equally unlovable, with his bulbous nose, flabby face, and downturned mouth; and was equally defiant about Biko's death: "The world can do its damnedest."[136]

We have a strange addendum to this most awful of race killings. Biko's close friend and biographer Donald Woods—on whom Richard Attenborough based his film *Cry Freedom* (1987)—describes meeting

133. (Soudien, 2012)
134. Jones is *coloured*.
135. He was born Welsh and given up for adoption to Afrikaans parents. (These days no European babies travel to South Africa to be adopted.)
136. Smuts used similar tough language in defending his suppression of African resistance (i.e., Bulhoek massacre of 1921).

Jimmy Kruger in 1969 and then again (at Kruger's home in Pretoria) for an informal meeting in the early '70s. Woods made a request: "I want to speak to you about a friend of mine, Steve Biko." Kruger's response was, as Woods described it, curious. "He lifted both hands to his head and lifted both feet off the floor in a gesture of comic consternation. 'Ooh!' he said. 'My God, Steve Biko! He's all tied up in knots. I know all about Mr Biko. He is a most dangerous man for the country.' "[137]

Jimmy Kruger had every reason to fear Biko's ideology. By the 1970s, black pride and black solidarity were making things difficult for the apartheid government. In response to the worldwide revulsion with apartheid, the government had rebranded its policy as *separate development*, dividing the mass of Africans into discrete ethnic groups and giving each a *Bantustan*. This was the actual word they used in the late '40s to describe fiefdoms for African ethnolinguistic groups. By the 1960s, the word *Bantustan* was being used derisively to criticize these sham homelands for what they were: cover for denying Africans rights in their own country. The Bantu Homelands Citizenship Act (1970) denied Africans their South African citizenship on the grounds they should seek them in their own *homelands*. None of these *homelands* was ever recognized by major powers.

This was indigenous rule ... by any expedient necessary. Each ethnolinguistic group had its *homeland*: QwaQwa for the Basotho people, Lebowa for the Bapedi, Transkei and Ciskei for the Xhosa, Kwazulu for the Zulu, Bophuthatswana for the Tswana, Gazankulu for the Tsonga, KaNgwane for the Swazi, Venda for the Venda, and KwaNdebele for the Ndebele. Four were granted *independence* and three, including Kwazulu, were given *autonomy*.[138] The Mathanzimas ruled Transkei, Sebe ruled Ciskei, Mphephu ruled Venda, and Mangope

---

137. (Woods, 1978, p. 85)
138. This is the old spelling of KwaZulu.

ruled Bophuthatswana, home of Sun City.[139] Chief Gatsha Buthelezi ruled Kwazulu, although he resisted attempts by the apartheid government to declare it *independent*.

These ethnolinguistic groups were the justification for the homeland system, which by 1960 was the white state's last gambit. In 1948, they had declared the white Afrikaner people a nation worthy of a country. Afrikaner nationalist thinkers like the influential Hendrik Verwoerd, prime minister from 1958–1966, could not rightly deny nationhood to other groupings. The government would have to buy up white farmland and make nations for them.

The homeland policy meant paying for ten separate fiefdoms, each with a Big Man supported by a small African petit bourgeois class. African polities were already poor and weak; they had little chance of creating a Wakanda in the bushveld on apartheid scraps. The black liberation movement knew this and refused to participate in the system.

If Verwoerd had thrown real money and better land at the *Bantustan solution*, it may have worked. In truth, the idea was muddled and expedient from the start. According to some it was a crime against humanity, with millions forcibly removed from their homes.[140]

By the early 1980s, Buthelezi was quoted in the newspaper saying, "The present government is evil in many ways." In the same newspaper, George Mathanzima, brother to Transkei's president, said, "The collective will of mankind is revulsed and they dread the bitter and cruel consequences of the race pogroms that have been perpetrated in Southern Africa in the name of Western Christian civilization."[141]

Homeland leader George Mathanzima, known by many as an apartheid proxy, railed in a speech from the early 1980s:

139. Mathanzima is also spelt *Matanzima*, depending on which brother one is referring to.
140. By some estimates, eleven million South Africans were forced to leave their homes and move to "black areas" during apartheid.
141. I have a PDF of the newspaper report in my possession.

The voices of the Xhosas who fought no less than nine wars of resistance against foreign aggression; of the Sothos who retreated and fought in the mountain fortresses on Thaba-Bosiu, of the Zulus who took a valiant stand on Blood River, of the Tswanas and other African national groups who laid down their lives in defence of the fatherland; of the dead of Langa and Sharpeville; of Soweto, of Mapetla, of Steve Biko and countless other patriots who died in prisons, gallows and detentions are now rising into a shrill voice and saying Enough; there will be no more. The entire world is saying to South Africa Enough . . .

Of all people, why was George Mathanzima playing the indigenous race card against his political masters? Mathanzima was related to Mandela; they were Xhosa royalty. The decision to run a Bantustan was a tactical move; the long game was indigenous deliverance. In the 1980s, the long game arrived, now it was time to redeem Hintsa, Maqoma, Dingaan, Makhanda, Mogale, and the other defeated chiefs.

Whites handed over power in 1994 not because they had been beaten on the battlefield or because they had run out of money. They handed over power to Africans because the story of white power was no longer valid. After the 1960s, there was a new story holding the Western imagination captive.

A hundred years ago it was obvious, even to many Africans, that Africa was generally tribal, and that Europe was generally civilized. The shock was that *civilization*, a mostly benign force, was used as justification to conquer Africans, take their land, and turn them into servants. There was also the justifiable suspicion from Africans that whites were not interested in the high ideals of their own civilization, and would always find a way to gang up with each other to oppress Africans. This suspicion has not disappeared.

DISTINCT RACE-CULTURES, DISTINCT POLITICS

The electoral shorthand for South Africa's racial division is *ANC versus DA*. South African minorities vote DA in similar proportion to what African Americans vote for the Democratic Party—about 90 per cent. No matter the DA's overwhelming support from whites, Indians, and *coloureds*, these minorities constitute less than one in five of the overall population, i.e., about 11.5 million out of sixty million.[142] You only need 60 per cent of Africans to turn out for the ANC, and they have a majority. This is more-or-less what happens, ensuring that the minorities are unlikely to ever enjoy real political representation at the national level.

The explicit political differences between the ANC and DA are of little significance. It's not their politics, it's the different cultures of the parties and the race of leaders that animate the electorate. After all, *people vote by group, not conviction.*[143] Whites simply trust that when DA leader John Steenhuisen laments the corrosive effects of corruption, he is being sincere and would rectify corruption if he were in

---

142. (Statista, 2021)
143. (Haidt, 2012)

power. By contrast, when an African politician in the ANC laments corruption, the minorities fear that he speaks in platitudes: even if he were sincere, the culture of his organization would not let him take serious action. There is something defeated in this. Here is Helen Zille writing on Facebook about today's great anti-corruption judicial show, the Zondo Commission into State Capture:

> Many South Africans are asking why, despite the evidence before the Zondo Commission, none of the most corrupt politicians identified have yet been sent to jail. I have come to the sad conclusion that it is BECAUSE of the Zondo Commission. I am not for a moment suggesting that Judge Zondo, Deputy Chief Justice, is doing anything wrong. He is chairing the Commission well. It is because of the existence of the commission.

> All the horrifying testimony that pours out every day should be presented to a properly constituted Court of Law, where the evidence can be tested, and if verified, used to convict and jail the corrupt.

> Instead, mind-boggling allegations and evidence of corruption pour out on a weekly basis, giving the public an illusion that "something" is being done, when in effect it is just a passing parade. It is surely plausible to draw the conclusion that the ANC wants to create the "illusion" that something is being done about corruption without actually sending anyone too senior to jail. I am now moving from skepticism to cynicism.[144]

Whites, Indians, and *coloureds* can vote all they like for the DA and against a hopelessly corrupt ruling party, but the effect is limited because there are too few of them to make an electoral impact. Effectively, our political system (straight proportional representation)

---

144. (Zille, 2021) I have removed some sentences from the original.

gives the country to whoever can rouse the African vote. The ANC is incentivised to play to its racial bloc. We are in a sectarian electoral stitch-up, as we were under white rule, but this time it's majoritarian.

Renowned South African historian Hermann Giliomee laments that the 1994 settlement was based on majority rule, with no concession to minority race group representation. It was thought that the white rulers would never bow to the one-man-one-vote principle. But they were under heavy international pressure to do so. As Giliomee puts it, "By 1970 ... most developed nations now insisted that democracy on the basis of universal franchise was the solution to any difficult problem."[145] Giliomee cites former diplomat and leader of Britain's Liberal Democrats, Paddy Ashdown, who gleaned some lessons from his involvement in Yugoslavia's transition after the fall of communism. According to Ashdown, "security and stability come first, then a well-functioning legal system and only then democracy."[146] As Giliomee wryly notes, "This was a lesson the American and the British learnt at great cost in Iraq. The present South African government still has to learn it."[147]

Why was African majority rule foisted on South Africa? In 1994, I was one of the people who were happy that it had been foisted on us. It was a proud day for South Africa when we redeemed the promise of democracy. The ballot box had won out over the bullet.

It was also a hasty compromise from all parties—one that did not account for our race reality. It was hoped that with a wave of the *democratic wand*, race politics would disappear.

One of my solutions to this racial Gordian Knot is to cut through it with a new concept, *race-culture*, which is sufficiently nuanced to account for the complexities of group identity. It is likely that the

145. (Giliomee, 2016)
146. (Giliomee, 2016)
147. (Giliomee, 2016)

antagonism between the world's different race-cultures will continue to animate geopolitics and domestic politics for centuries to come. And that we are better off setting the parameters of mutual respect between the world's race-cultures, instead of pretending race does not exist.

Before 1994, South Africa had its own culture wars within the European race-culture, with whites split about race. Although liberal and radical-left whites were always a minority voice during the years of white supremacy, they could often count on influential figures in the media, the academy, the Church, and even some in business. This is much like the US today, where conservative and centrist whites greatly outnumber progressives, while progressives are often influential within institutions.

South Africa's culture war among whites is now irrelevant. Left, right or centre, everyone from the minorities dreads the ruin of African rule and the devolution of the state to rent seekers. We can argue all day on Facebook, but everyone knows that when the hordes attack, we'll be on the same side of the barricade.

As mentioned, the most multiracial party in the country is the DA, a political home for minorities and moderate Africans. Africanists typify the DA as a *white party in the pay of white capital*. Influential DA leader Helen Zille, among many others, was keen to change that and bring in more black leaders, proving that her party is a home for *all* who share her liberal values (of the classical British variety).

In 2014, Zille persuaded her old friend Mamphela Ramphele to be the DA's presidential candidate in the upcoming general election. Ramphele was Steve Biko's lover, and had two children with him. Zille was also connected to Biko; as a young journalist working for the liberal newspaper *The Rand Daily Mail*, she helped expose the apartheid government's cover-up of his murder.

Ramphele is a medical doctor who was vice-chancellor of the

University of Cape Town and a managing director at the World Bank. She was the ideal face for a party trying to deracialize its image. In late January 2014, the *Mail & Guardian*, a newspaper, published an article about the political partnership between Zille and Ramphele.[148] Zille told the paper that having Ramphele on the ballot paper for the DA would, "help remove the opportunistic use of the race card" against her party; and that because Ramphele was black, she had more latitude to speak up. As Zille put it:

> It's difficult for me to say race should not be the issue, because people immediately say: "Oh yes, you are white and of course you would say that" … but when Dr Ramphele gets up there and says race is not the issue, fixing education is the issue; fixing healthcare is the issue; getting land reform right is the issue … then people don't focus on their race as they do with me.

Ramphele concurred, saying: "this is a historic moment where we are going to take away the excuse of race and challenge the ANC to be judged on its performance." This very comment was just what Zille meant about Ramphele being able to say things she couldn't, such as the fact that race should not be an excuse for failure.

Nelson Mandela had died less than two months before this dramatic political announcement. Among minorities and moderate Africans, the rainbow promise of Mandela was also dying with every passing day of Zuma's misrule. Mandela's death was one of the reasons that Mamphela and Zille had decided to turn a personal friendship into a political partnership. As Zille put it, "Madiba (Mandela) has passed on; there is a huge cry for bringing people together and ensuring we rekindle the vision that Madiba had." Ramphele echoed this sentiment: "It is time for those who fought for freedom to enable the transcendence

---

148. (Makinana, 2014)

of the politics of divide," and "We want to honour his [Mandela's] legacy by taking the country forward by focusing on tomorrow and not yesterday."

What would black-consciousness icon Steve Biko have made of the situation: his lover-comrade giving credibility to white political power? Perhaps Ramphele was thinking about that when she reneged on the deal only a week after the announcement. Strangely, Ramphele wanted to lead her own party, Agang SA, as well as the DA in the elections, which—as Zille pointed out—was "unconstitutional" and "electoral nonsense."[149] Later, Ramphele *explained* the reason for the breakdown of the deal: "Some cannot or will not transcend party politics. The time for this was not right. We see people trapped in old-style race-based politics."

Parachuting Ramphele in at the last minute to head up a mostly white party is the very epitome of race-based politics. Zille was playing the same race games she criticized others for.

Ramphele is one of four high-profile African leaders who were meant to deracialize the DA but somehow had the opposite effect. Lindiwe Mazibuko, a Swazi by birth, was elected DA parliamentary leader in 2011. Within a few years, she became unpopular with the DA caucus and with DA leader Helen Zille, resigning in 2014 to study at Harvard.

In the beginning, Zille boosted Mazibuko. According to a reporter writing in 2014, "Zille said she had never in her life done as much to advance the career of any individual as she had done for Mazibuko."[150] Given Zille's disillusionment with Mazibuko's performance, she may have regretted putting so much hope in her. But it didn't stop her from boosting another rising black star, Mmusi Maimane. Those around her

---

149. (news24, 2014)
150. (news24, 2014)

were concerned about the pattern, prompting Zille to deny "that the same pattern is developing with Maimane."[151]

Thanks in part to Zille, Maimane was elected as the DA's parliamentary leader in late May 2014. In 2015, Maimane continued his rise in the party, succeeding Zille as DA leader in a landslide vote and becoming the party's first black leader and, at only thirty-five years of age, their youngest ever leader. In 2016 Mazibuko endorsed Maimane's campaign to fight racism within the DA and promote more diversity. She told an interviewer: "The party should reflect on a culture that isolates black members and leaders."[152] Notwithstanding Maimane's leadership, Mazibuko criticized the DA for a brains' trust that, she believed, was made up almost entirely of white males.[153]

Maimane's tenure proved that the race card can be played against black people who are seen to be soft on racism. When party stalwarts Diane Kohler-Barnard and Helen Zille faced criticism for politically incorrect posts on social media, Maimane took flak from the left for not being tough enough on them.

Maimane could not bridge South Africa's race divide and found himself sandwiched between whites who feared he was selling out the DA's liberal values and blacks who accused him of being an Uncle Tom. The 2019 general elections saw the DA lose ground. Maimane—facing a probable loss in the upcoming DA leadership elections—announced his resignation, saying, "Despite my best efforts, the DA is not the vehicle best suited to take forward the vision of building one South Africa for all." Maimane, who is a lay pastor at his church, left politics to go into business.

Herman Mashaba, a business tycoon who founded South Africa's biggest hair brand, Black Like Me, also enjoyed initial support from

---

151. (news24, 2014)
152. (Clarke, 2016)
153. (Clarke, 2016)

Zille, before resigning from the DA in October 2019. Mashaba epitomizes the African self-reliance success story, having defied apartheid and poverty to become a millionaire. His values are true-blue conservative: anti-immigrants, pro-free-enterprise, pro-family.

From 2016 to 2019, he represented the DA as the mayor of Johannesburg. When Helen Zille returned as federal council chairperson, Mashaba resigned from the DA, making good on his threat to leave the party if "right-wing elements took over." He announced, "I am gravely concerned that the DA I signed up to is no longer the DA that has emerged out of this weekend's Federal Council."[154]

Mashaba (for the DA) was running Johannesburg in coalition with the EFF. Despite their ideological differences, Mashaba got on rather well with the EFF—suspiciously so for the white *pure liberals* who feared the party was compromising its core values.[155] When Maimane and Mashaba resigned, Malema expressed support for them on social media, coming to the inevitable conclusion they were the victims of a racist conspiracy.

In his resignation letter, posted on *Twitter*, Mashaba stated:

> The election of Helen Zille as the Chairperson of the Federal Council represents a victory for people in the DA who stand diametrically opposed to my beliefs and value system, and I believe those of most South Africans of all backgrounds. I cannot reconcile myself with a group of people who believe that race is irrelevant in the discussion of inequality and poverty in South Africa in 2019.[156]

Perhaps Mashaba has a point. Not only in South Africa but the

---

154. (*The Citizen*, 2019)
155. Reporters used this term (*pure liberals*) to describe the mostly white DA leaders who organised against the likes of Maimane and Mashaba.
156. (Mashaba, 2019)

world over, Africans and people of African origin are disproportion-ately impoverished. Race (or *race-culture* as I would prefer to call it) surely has something to do with the story.

But why did Mashaba label Zille *right-wing*? Across all the mark-ers of ideological positioning, Mashaba himself is thoroughly right-wing. A profile of Mashaba starts with this line: "Herman Mashaba is a millionaire tycoon, an ideological libertarian, and self-proclaimed 'capitalist crusader' who lectures his listeners about the evils of big government and minimum wage."[157] Mashaba and Helen Zille should be ideological bedfellows, but Zille, who is of German-Jewish origin, has a fearsome correctitude about her that doesn't sit well with all types.[158]

Black and white DA members agree on everything, except for race. White liberals want to pretend race doesn't exist in any real sense and that, in King's immortal words, it's about the content of the character, not the colour of the skin.

On the surface, all four of these African leaders should have fitted in well with the DA. But you can't boost black people to win black support and then complain when they do things you don't like. You are either a real leader or you are a token. After this string of failures, Zille realised that she had been dancing to someone else's tune.

Around the time of Mashaba's resignation she rued the fact that the DA had engaged in the "ANC/EFF's race narrative arena."[159] The problem for Zille is that there isn't much of an alternative to the left's race narrative. Zille is up against people who can wear their racial heritage as a badge of pride; she can't—not without alienating the bulk

---

157. (York, 2016)
158. I once met Zille at a cross-dressing party thrown by my brother-in-law; I will never forget her dogged concentration and patience in affixing my brother's bra, which had come loose.
159. (IOL, 2019)

of the African vote. In a tweet, Zille responded to a meme, "When you want to become woke but it isn't enough," with, "It will never be enough. It is known as feeding steaks to a crocodile in the hope that it will become vegetarian."[160]

Despite these racial setbacks and the fact that the DA now has a white man in charge, it still has some African leadership and some support from African voters. Dr Mpho Phalatse, a DA candidate, was elected as Johannesburg's mayor in late 2021. The DA only won 26 per cent of the vote in Johannesburg, but Phalatse enjoyed support from Mashaba's new party ActionSA and the EFF. These two parties refused a coalition with the DA, but they voted to make Dr Phalatse, a black woman, mayor ... and then a year later tried to get rid of her because (according to the DA) they want to protect their patronage networks. There's a tribal thing going on that's very hard to defend against.

As a privileged minority, whites—and those seen to be in league with them—will always lose when powerful actors play the race representation game. Race representation is the *AK-47* of the culture warriors on the left, who explain difference in outcome as the inevitable result of a racially oppressive system. Their solution is to recalibrate the values of our culture according to *race equity*: the numbers game of boosting blacks into positions of responsibility. Their solution cannot work because reframing standards demeans the very people you're trying to boost, as American economist Glenn Loury explains:

> It's undignified for black people to be reliant on special dispensation ... to be included into the most valued venues of society as a permanent way of doing business ... That's not equality; that's being a ward; that's being a client. You're being taken care of; you're being covered for ... there is a corruption of the soul here attendant to accepting special dispensation as if

160. (Zille, 2017)

it were your right because of something that happened—not to you—not even to your parents—something that happened to your ancestors long since gone. You buy into a narrative of permanent injury and then you walk around with your hand out expecting to be treated specially; afforded a special privilege as an entitlement and you call that equality? That's not equality. [161]

Race inequality cannot be fixed by race equity. In 1994, South Africa's European race-culture surrendered political control of the country to the African race-culture. That wasn't the idea though. The idea was that an overarching democratic culture would supersede all race-cultures and solve our race crisis. That did not happen. Not by a long shot.

In South Africa—perhaps in America too—race is bigger than politics and it's possibly bigger even than culture. Our current shame is that in an age of civil rights for all, the races still organize themselves into opposing political blocs. This contradicts our humanist assumption that class and economic mode are more important than race in determining the contours of society. At university we're taught to believe that class and personality—not race—determine sociopolitical identity. Our actual experience of this country proves that it's the other way around. Race-culture is the dominant feature of our sociopolitical landscape. That's why politics is such a tame affair in Scandinavian countries, which only become animated and divided on subjects like immigration.

The ANC is the political embodiment of the African race-culture in South Africa. Africans do not have a rich history of state-building and have had to borrow ideologies to bring coherence to their race-culture project. The ANC's rhetoric and policy documents follow Marxist

---

161. (Loury, 2022)

syntax, with an anti-colonial flavour: *The state as vanguard for indigenous restitution against vested white interests unjustly accumulated over centuries of white supremacist rule.*

This is wrong. We didn't only dominate and oppress, we also brought with us a civilization worth keeping … I think.

OUR WEIRD CIVILIZATION

In a society that has abolished every kind of adventure,
the only adventure that remains is to abolish society.

—Graffiti (May 1968 Paris youth revolts)[162]

*C*ivilization comes from *civitas*, the citizenry. What binds individual citizens to the *civitas*? Shared agreement articulated in written contract. Reading and writing are the sacred acts of civilization by which we transcend the limits of space and time, commune with the dead and the not-yet-born, and by which we express our sacred inner world.

By the late 1960s, the European race-culture was in some turmoil. A divisive overseas war and youth protests rocked the US and Europe. It was the fate of Kenneth Clark, a British art historian, to set the record straight with his thirteen-part docuseries, *Civilisation: A Personal View* (1969). Clark was inspired to make the series after David Attenborough had dropped the word *civilisation* into a conversation they were having about a new show.

Clark cared about art. During the Nazi Blitz he trucked Britain's art treasures to caves in Wales.[163] *Civilisation* gave bewildered Western

162. (Meis, 2016)
163. (Meis, 2016)

audiences a reason to care about their culture.[164]

In the first episode, Clark makes a startling admission: "What is civilisation? I don't know. I can't define it in abstract terms yet." Then he offers some important context:

> Looking at those great works of Western man and remembering all that he has achieved in philosophy, poetry, science, lawmaking, it does seem hard to believe that European civilization can ever vanish. And yet you know it has happened once. All the life-giving activities that we lump together as civilization have been obliterated once in Western Europe when the Barbarians ran over the Roman Empire. For two centuries, the heart of European civilisation almost stopped beating. We got through by the skin of our teeth. In the last few years, we've developed an uneasy feeling that this could happen again. And advanced thinkers, who even in Roman times thought it fine to gang up on the Barbarians, have begun to question if civilization is worth preserving. Well, this is why it seems to me a good moment to look at some of the ways that man has shown himself to be an intelligent, creative, orderly, and compassionate animal.[165]

Clark's series was not about civilization generally, but about European civilization, the very idea of which is under attack from the academy. In the penultimate episode, *The Fallacies of Hope*, Clark tells us: "We have a long, rough, voyage ahead of us and I can't say how it will end. Because it isn't over yet. We are still the offspring of the romantic movement and still victims of the fallacies of hope."[166] As he puts it: "In the 18th century philosophers had attempted to tidy up

---

164. *Civilisation* came out in Britain in 1969, the year I was born, and was released on PBS in the US in 1970.
165. (*Civilisation: A Personal View*, 1969)
166. (*Civilisation: A Personal View*, 1969)

human society through the use of reason ... towards the end of the 18th century, as rational argument declined, vivid assertion took its place."[167]

One of the most vivid of assertions of the romantic movement, as Clark attests, comes from the Swiss-French philosopher Jean-Jacques Rousseau (1712–1778): *Man was born free and everywhere he is in chains.* On the upside, this type of thinking helped slough off the *huge mass of torpid tradition* that weighed on European society in the 18th century.[168] On the downside, the granting of ever more freedoms to ever more people has meant handing over the culture to thirteen-year-old girls from California.

Our exaggerated emphasis on individual freedoms has made us *WEIRD* (Western, educated, industrialised, rich, and democratic). This acronym was coined by Harvard professor Joseph Henrich in *The WEIRDest People in the World: How the West Became Psychologically Peculiar and Particularly Preposterous* (2020). Jonathan Haidt, author and social psychologist, summarizes his research on the phenomenon as: "WEIRD societies are statistical outliers on many psychological measures, including measures of moral psychology."

Haidt is influenced by the social psychologist Richard Shweder, who in 1993 researched the moral attitudes of folk in Bhubaneswar, northeast India.[169] Shweder and his team produced a paper titled, "The 'Big Three' of Morality (Autonomy, Community, Divinity) and the 'Big Three' Explanations of Suffering".[170] According to Shweder, morality is how people deal with suffering, be it psychological, socio-political, biomedical, moral, or divine suffering. We soften these

167. (*Civilisation: A Personal View*, 1969)
168. Clark's phrase from Episode 12.
169. The paper I draw on for this book includes work by other researchers (as cited); in this chapter I reference Shweder singularly, noting that in truth he headed up a team of researchers and writers.
170. (Shweder, et al., 1997)

sufferings through our commitments to autonomy, community, and divinity. Almost universally, humans have a sense that, "It is good to have personal autonomy and control (autonomy), it is good to be part of an organized community and to have an identity or place within its social structure (community), and it is good to experience communication and to be on speaking terms with the divine (divinity)."[171]

It is not hard to see that Western liberals tend to *background* the moral foundations of community and divinity, and to *foreground* autonomy.[172] Our six-cylinder moral vehicle is only firing on two cylinders.

The West has all its moral eggs in the autonomy basket, infusing our institutions with a "harm-rights-and-justice code ... with its emphasis on the individual's claim to self-interest and noninterference."[173]

It's not that autonomy is a bad thing in itself, it's only bad if it crowds out other important moral considerations, like community, which depends on our commitment to what Shweder calls *feudal ethics*: duty, honour, chivalry, respect, ritualized humility, etc. You need these values to promote social interdependence, the very glue that holds society together. If it's true that South Africa is coming apart at the seams, then it's because these values have been undermined, thanks in part to our *WEIRD* constitution.

You would guess that South Africa's constitution would commonly mention words related to harm-prevention, words like *rights*, *care*, *fairness*, and *freedom*. You would be right. *Rights* are mentioned 111 times; *fairness* is mentioned eleven times, as is *care*. *Freedom* appears no fewer than thirty-four times in the South African constitution. What about words that have to do with community obligations: *honour, respect, loyalty, responsibility*?

Responsibility, in terms of how it relates to the duties of ordinary

---

171. (Shweder, et al., 1997)
172. Shweder's terms.
173. (Shweder, et al., 1997)

citizens is mentioned only once in our constitution: "All citizens are equally subject to the duties and responsibilities of citizenship." There is zero detail on what that responsibility looks like or how the irresponsible citizen is to be sanctioned.

Loyalty is not mentioned at all. *Duty*, other than the five times it is used in a technical sense, is only mentioned once, this in reference to the duty of the state, not the citizen. *Honour* is mentioned only three times in the constitution and is disrespected routinely by our state officials, who swear to "respect and uphold the Constitution and all other law" and to "hold office with honour and dignity." *Obedience* is mentioned nine times, all of them in the phrase, "obedience to the Constitution."

What about words that indicate our foundational value of divinity and the sacred world, or words that point to its negation: *pollution, decay, corruption,* and *degradation*? *God* (mentioned nine times) is only used perfunctorily in oaths and prayer. There is no *sanctity* or *sacred*—certainly no *enchanted* and no *devotion*. *Pollution* is mentioned four times but only in the sense of environmental (biomedical) pollution. *Decay* is not mentioned at all, nor is *corruption*, a word journalists cannot do without in this country.

What about *degradation*? It is only mentioned twice, once as in a child's right not to experience, "abuse and degradation." The other time as in environmental protection: "Everyone has the right to prevent pollution and degradation." Interestingly, even the natural environment is turned into an extension of our sacred self, whose whims, more so than the environment itself, must be respected. Rousseau would have been proud.

Liberalism reduces the stock of moral capital inadvertently, Haidt tells us. Never mind moral capital, what about the economy? Is it possible that we have an economy that's all about preventing harm and looking after people, and not about dutybound men and women building things of utility and beauty?

In terms of employment and job-creation, our biggest sector is community and social services, which employs 3.26 million; manufacturing is fourth on the list, employing only 1.3 million.[174] By way of contrasting example, in Vietnam agriculture, forestry, and fishing are at the top (17.7 million people employed); followed by manufacturing (11.3 million) and then wholesale, retail, and vehicle repair (7.3 million).[175]

South African society is skewed, over-emphasizing rights, care, freedom, and justice at the expense of livelihood and purpose. We will not build a civilization in South Africa unless we develop some vision of our sacred interdependence as citizens.

Ian McGilchrist, a British philosopher and neuroscientist, introduces a startling idea— one aimed sharply at our European race-culture and its obsession with personal autonomy. The two hemispheres of our brain, left and right, represent and embody distinct personalities. He typifies the divide as one between *The Master and His Emissary* (the title of his book released in 2009). Our right hemisphere (*Master*) is the more spiritual and holistic side of us, able to appreciate reality both in immediacy and contextually. The left hemisphere (*Emissary*) operates in an abstract world, partly of its own making. The left-hemisphere *Emissary* needs the right-hemisphere *Master* to set the context and sum up the meaning of the occasion before it can go out and manipulate reality for its ends. McGilchrist suggests our race-culture achievements have come at a cost:

> Our talent for division, for seeing the parts, is of staggering importance—second only to our capacity to transcend it, in

174. (Gala, 2022)
175. (Nguyen, 2021)

order to see the whole. These gifts of the left hemisphere have helped us achieve nothing less than civilization itself ... Even if we could abandon them, which of course we can't, we would be fools to do so, and would come off infinitely the poorer. There are siren voices that call us to do exactly that, certainly to abandon clarity and precision (which, in any case, importantly depend on both hemispheres), and I want to emphasize that I am passionately opposed to them. We need the ability to make fine discriminations, and to use reason appropriately. But these contributions need to be made in the service of something else, that only the right hemisphere can bring. Alone they are destructive. And right now they may be bringing us close to forfeiting the civilization they helped to create.[176]

What's it like to see the world through the left hemisphere as opposed to the right? It's neurotic, grasping, and hyper-competitive. It's the trap of calibrating the world in terms of the metaphor of the sacred self. Could Shweder and McGilchrist have come upon the same crisis but from different fields of study?

In the West we foreground autonomy, and we background community and divinity. In other words, we read the Old Testament through the lens of the New Testament. Like when your friend tells you, *I stopped coming to church because it just wasn't working for me.* Finding a religion that *works for me* is what we do in the West.

The bad news is that Europe's great achievements of the Enlightenment and the Age of Science and Reason were built on a warped psychology. This derangement helped deliver an unworkable political solution for South Africa, one that ignored the realities of human nature and compromised the cause of state-building. Using any amount of plain common sense, it should have been obvious that what

---

176. (McGilchrist, 2009)

we have got is what we were always going to get.

White South Africa, as a cultural satellite of the West, was under pressure to make the leap to a pluralistic society based on classical liberal values. This was all well and good. But in the West, and in South Africa too, we began to repudiate those values for being *systemically* racist. While black leaders were finding their voice and laying claim to their role as beacons of African civilization, Europeans—inspired by the strange maunderings of French existentialism—jumped off the cliff.

JM Coetzee, South Africa's most important writer, has won two Booker Prizes and one Nobel Prize for literature. Coetzee is your existential father who wakes up your little six-year-old self at 4 a.m. on Christmas morning, rips his fake beard off and shouts, "LOOK, SON! IT'S REALLY ME! SANTA CLAUS IS BULLSHIT!"

His *Waiting for the Barbarians* (1980) takes its title from a poem (1900) by Constantine Cavafy set in the time of Ancient Greece. The poem is about a city-state that fears conquest from barbarians camped somewhere outside the gates. Cavafy's barbarians are really a convenient threat to justify repression by self-serving rulers, perhaps the way some governments today justify their repression as *dealing with terrorism.*

But in Coetzee's novel, the barbarians are a genuine threat to the state. The protagonist (*the magistrate*) is a tired old man caught between his duty to *the Empire* and his recognition of the barbarians as equals. He is uncomfortable about upholding an unjust order, but also disapproves of the barbarian way of life. His enthusiasm for archaeological excavation has him musing: "Do I really look forward to the triumph of the barbarian way: intellectual torpor, slovenliness, tolerance of disease and death? If we were to disappear, would the barbarians spend the afternoons excavating our ruins?"

Coetzee journeys to the heart of what's troubling sensitive white South Africans. Which is: *I care for Africans and want to see them flourish, but I don't like what has happened in postcolonial Africa. I'm deeply pessimistic about African governance, and I secretly think they'd be better off living under benign white rule.*

JM Coetzee should be a treasured citizen of our land, but instead he moved to Adelaide, Australia. A move that came three years after he published *Disgrace* (1999), for which he earned his second Booker Prize.

The plot of *Disgrace* pivots around the rape by three black men of the white protagonist's daughter. The liberal daughter sees it as her duty to forgive. She does not report the crime to the police, preferring that the elders in the black community deal with the situation themselves. Some decades before *Disgrace*, Coetzee wrote in one of his novels, "What are we doing here, what if the whole project of civilizing the place was misconceived from the start?" Coetzee was interested in the problem of whites in Africa; that we will always feel alienated from Africans and Africa. He has a point. Whites don't like being ruled by a people so different from them, especially if it entails putting up with African state failure and the contrivances of patronage politics. Is this what Coetzee was exiling himself from when he left South Africa?

About the time he left, I remember reading something he said on race relations where he cycled back to his earlier theme about the *failed* project to spread European civilization in Africa. He made the startling claim that the economic modes of Africans differ fundamentally from ours, noting that the African pastoralist tradition of cattle-raiding has its echo in contemporary political expression. This may seem racist, but Coetzee is suggesting that we should not judge our European ways as being intrinsically better than non-African ways.

War and totalitarianism in the twentieth century produced a new type of thinker, one less certain about the European civilizing mission. Now universities in the West are dominated by people hostile to the idea of *Western Civilization*. Jordan Peterson has addressed the problem in great depth, arguing convincingly that we cannot rubbish the advances of our civilization and hope to get away with it. But progressive humanities' departments seem to be preaching that very line, caricaturing our highest culture as a grand project of exploitation and colonial plunder.

Coetzee is willing to concede the point to progressives, taking their narrative to its ominous end. Rape is perhaps not as bad as we make it out to be, as long as we contextualize it within the overall story of the clash between two *equals*: European modernity and African tribalism. Coetzee left South Africa in 2002, as Mbeki was hitting his Africanist stride and alienating whites by portraying the country in racial terms: *rich whites versus poor blacks*. We may as well have been stuck in 1900, when the Pan-African Conference declared, "The problem of the twentieth century is the problem of the colour line!"[177] A sentiment Mbeki approvingly referenced.

Coetzee had enough of the colour line, and so he moved. In his wake, he left a dismal idea of Africans as culturally (perhaps even preternaturally) driven to raid and pillage.[178] Seven years after Coetzee moved to Australia Jacob Zuma became president, teaming up with the Guptas to set up those networks of state pillage. Notwithstanding some excoriating editorials, Zuma's crimes attracted a muted response from the African intelligentsia and African students. Fifty years on from the 1960s, we were still being haunted by the *indigenous rule by any means necessary* idea—the one that sank Liberia and Zimbabwe. Zuma got away with it by playing the *100 per cent Zulu Boy* card, a

---

177. He references it in the same piece where I have quoted him here.
178. I do not have the exact reference, but his edgy comments about so-called African economic ways were reported in the mainstream press.

variation on the race card. [179]

He worked with the enterprising Gupta family to subvert South Africa's net of anti-corruption laws, looting billions from the fiscus: a flow of cash making its way down the chain of his patronage network, out to Dubai. Radical students were not interested in the *Zuptas*, instead taking on dead white men. Cecil John Rhodes—respected by many Africans in his day—was targeted over a century after his death. [180] The *#RhodesMustFall* movement brought the university to a standstill, with black students demanding that his statue be removed from their sight.

This accomplished, they lost interest in dead white men and got down to business with the *#FeesMustFall* movement, by which middle-class African students protested having to pay college fees, which are already subsidized by the state. Should whites and black moderates have protected Rhodes' statue from the hordes? White society in South Africa was built on everything he stood for. If we couldn't be bothered to defend Rhodes' reputation, then—as Coetzee asked— what are we still doing here?

If you want to keep your civilization, there's a line you must defend. We don't know where that line is anymore and our greatest writers can't be bothered to help us draw that line, reveling instead in the crazy irony of it all. A hundred years ago, we could with far more certainty see the line. In the past we defended our civilization behind ramparts and city walls, hurling rocks at the hordes with our trebuchets. Now the barbarian is within us and all around us. How do we know who is virtuous and dignified, and who is an animal dressed up in fine clothes?

World ideology, with its heady emphasis on progress, is unrecognizable from those far-off days of trebuchets lobbing rocks at hordes.

179. (Moya, 2006)
180. Willan notes that Rhodes' funeral (1902) was attended by thousands of Africans.

Yet it's not entirely clear if progressive race ideologies have delivered progress. In postcolonial Africa it is often the case that culture and civilization have been degraded, doing terrible damage to the cause of African dignity.

Speak to a liberal on this subject and it's obvious they're disillusioned that progress in politics does not necessarily lead to economic and institutional progress, and that race and culture usually matter more than politics. We naively thought democratic elections would magically produce a viable nation and solve the indignity of the black race; a goal that has proved near impossible to achieve.

THE WORLDWIDE INDIGNITY OF THE BLACK RACE

The end of apartheid in South Africa and civil rights victories in America were meant to solve our segregation problems for good. We were meant to become integrated as free and equal individuals within a tolerably fair social order. If this had happened, there would be no crisis in South Africa and no need for me to write this book.

Race is more intractable than we think. It is a partly genetic phenomenon that shapes social behaviour and sometimes determines, in broad terms, who we associate with and how we identify ourselves.

The worldwide *race crisis* is primarily about the problem that indigenous race-cultures in the South tend to fare poorly when competing against race-cultures in the West and the East.

As Nigerian journalist Chigozie Obioma puts it, "the worldwide indignity of the black race is the core reason why black people have remained synonymous with the denigrating experience of racism."[181] This is an interesting alternative to the standard view, which is that racism causes indignity. No, says Obioma, indignity causes racism.

181. (Obioma, 2016) I have paraphrased the original slightly.

Denying this fact only makes the situation worse, as Obioma explains:

> Black elites and activists across the world … have adopted a culture of verbal tyranny in which they shut down any effort to reason or criticize us [Nigerians] or black-majority nations by labelling such attempts as 'racism' or 'hate speech'. Thus … any suggestions that our race may indeed need to do something to remedy our situation will not be aired—not by the terrified people of other races. And anyone within our race who makes such a suggestion will be deemed weak and pandering or a sellout, as US President Barack Obama has repeatedly been called. Thus, no one will talk about the painful fact that most African and Caribbean nations have either failed or are about to collapse. [182]

We can easily prove Obioma's point—that indignity causes racism, with a thought experiment. Consider the example of Chinese immigrants to America. If a white American is racist towards a Chinese American, who cares? In the US, those of Chinese origin outcompete whites in business and the professions. They have little to be triggered about when some white trash racially demeans them. Because he belongs to a winning racial group, the racially abused Chinese person can shrug off the offence. After all, his people have proven that the racial slur of being inferior is untrue. He can simply block his ears and think on the *solid Chinese state* whence he originates. This is in stark contrast to the racially abused black person who, Obioma tells us, does not have a *solid black state* whence to draw dignity:

> Great men like Marcus Garvey, W.E.B. Du Bois, and Malcolm X all knew that a people is only respected when it has a nation worthy of respect. A man who lives in a shack cannot expect

---

182. (Obioma, 2016)

to be treated with respect at a palace. They knew that for us to reclaim power we must first reclaim dignity and that this comes through the construction of a solid black state with a demonstrable level of development and prosperity—and which can stand as a powerful advocate for the global black. Today, no such state exists.

Black Panther (2018) addresses the dignity deficit problem by way of fiction. The film is about Wakanda, a super-advanced southern African nation that pretends to be backward for fear of attracting unwanted attention. Within a couple of months of its release it had grossed a remarkable $1.3 billion worldwide, establishing itself as a cult hit, particularly among those of African descent. Some critics rejected its implication that Africans need to prove themselves as good Westerners to have their dignity restored.

Obioma laments that there are few African-run institutions that enjoy a reputation for world-beating excellence. There is no *Wakanda* in the real world. We don't have a polite answer as to why African states, as well as those run by other indigenous groups, tend to fare poorly in the things the modern world prizes: economic power, institutional efficiency, technological advancement. Sporting and entertainment prowess aside, people of African origin are badly under-represented in the fields that our world culture bows to—fields like business, science, and technology.

There is no African (or person of African descent) winner of a Nobel Prize for the sciences and only one for economics. There are three for literature and twelve for peace. Of the twenty-four poorest countries in the world, all but Afghanistan and Haiti are African. Interestingly, Ellen Johnson Sirleaf—Liberia's president from 2006 to 2018 and Africa's first elected female head of state—won the Nobel Peace Prize in 2011. This didn't do much good for Liberia, which is ranked the world's poorest country, with a gross national income of only $710 per person.[183]

Africa continues to attract a tiny proportion of foreign direct investment; according to the IMF the income gap between sub-Saharan Africa and the rest of the world is ever widening.[184] The technocrats tell us that you need $1.90 per day to escape the indignity of extreme poverty. By this formulation, however, about four hundred million Africans are *undignified*. By 2030, 90 per cent of the world's *undignified* will be sub-Saharan Africans.[185]

Progressives would not be so hyped about race if Africans were eating at humanity's top table.[186] Their solution is to level things up by knocking the privileged down. But for all the anti-racism hype from the '60s onwards there's been no reduction whatsoever in the *worldwide indignity of the black race*. It's worse now: back in 1960, Zambians were as rich as South Koreans, and much of Asia was poorer than Africa.

Today, humanitarians and progressives in the West are befuddled as to what to do with Africa. The big investors and financiers mostly avoid sub-Saharan Africa, leaving it to the humanitarians to engage with the continent.

Bill Gates is a *tech-humanitarian*. His mission statement, as per the Bill and Melinda Gates Foundation website, is: "We believe that by giving people the tools to lead healthy, productive lives, we can help them lift themselves out of poverty." These tools include "new farming

---

183. The Nobel is sometimes a booby prize for Africa. Ethiopia's president Abiy Ahmed won the Nobel Peace Prize in 2019, but now critics want it rescinded because of atrocities perpetrated amidst the current Tigray conflict.
184. (International Monetary Fund, 2021)
185. The Brookings Institution notes that between 1996 and 2011, the number of Africans living in poverty went from 358 million to 415 million; while between 2000 and 2015, the number of African dollar millionaires doubled, reaching 160,000 people.
186. I generally do not use "racism" to refer to the victimization of non-blacks.

technologies," "new jobs," and "new business opportunities."

Like white pioneers impressing a local chief with the shiny objects of their civilization, the Gates Foundation is doing the same with its own shiny objects: *new farming technologies, new jobs, new business opportunities.*

Our role as whites in Africa used to be defined by the idea that we had a superior civilization—one worth selling to the indigenous. That idea is now taboo, even to putative Christians like Bill and Melinda Gates. For all the good that Bill and Melinda Gates do, they cannot solve the African indignity crisis, which can only be solved by self-reliance.

In the documentary *Buddha in Africa* (2019), director Nicole Shafer follows the story of Enock, a Malawian orphan who is taken in by a Taiwanese Buddhist order called Amitofo Care Centre (ACC). The ACC is run by Master Hui Li, who is dedicated to bringing "Chinese Buddhist civilization to Africa." In a motivational talk to the kids, he goads them by drawing a clear line between what he offers and where they come from:

> Now that you are part of ACC, you must follow the Buddhist commandment and follow our ways. Because only in this way, the donors will continue to support us. You may decide you don't like it this way or don't want the opportunity to study abroad later [in Taiwan]. You don't want to learn about civilization and the advanced thoughts of the world. You prefer to go back to your tribes. You decide to leave ACC. I respect your choice. I wish you the best of luck.[187]

Master Hiu Li takes the Churchillian approach to cultural interaction. He promises poor Africans blood, toil, tears, and sweat in the vague hope of escaping poverty a generation down the line. Master

---

187. (*Buddha in Africa*, 2019)

Hiu Li tells destitute Malawians he will teach their children to become Chinese … like him. Some Malawians take him up on the offer and stay committed to the project for twenty years. Those kids who go through it now find themselves studying in Taiwan and readying themselves for a life in the East. If they stay in the East or within its institutions, they are far more likely to become middle-class. How does Master Hiu Lu do it? He remorselessly rams Chinese language, Buddhist religion, and Kung Fu form down the throats of his charges. Master Hui Li tells the youngsters they can either stay and *learn about civilization and the advanced thoughts of the world* or *go back to their tribes*.

Is it a bad thing to go back to your tribe? Not according to *Tribe*, a new South African magazine label catering to aspirant urban Africans.

Why does a magazine about black business aspiration call itself *Tribe*? No matter what white liberals make of our situation, there is a clear call from the African intelligentsia that blacks should draw a circle around their *tribe* and work towards its deliverance. A main feature in the rather flimsy hardcopy of *Tribe* (August 2022) is an interview with Professor Bonang Mohale, the chancellor of the University of the Free State, and president of Business Unity South Africa. Mohale is an academic and upstanding business leader. He typifies the contradictions inherent in being a successful African in South Africa. He is outspoken against the corruption and ineptitude of our state and yet his solution is not less tribal Africaness but more of it. He tells *Tribe*:

> The African way is looking at the son that is stealing the apricots from their neighbor's yard without permission … and not shaming them in public … but seating him under the Marula tree where his elders will teach him that his people have worked very hard in order for that tree to be fruitful. . . When he leaves there he has only one thought; I'm going to hold

my clan name in the highest esteem, I would never soil it and shame it.[188]

Leading Africans like Mohale manage to come across as being both conservative and radical at the same time. Remember Morgan Freeman (Principal Joe Clark) in *Lean on Me* (1989): "We are being crucified by a process that is turning blacks into a permanent underclass here, Frank. A permanent underclass!"[189] Mohale strikes a similarly shrill tone:

It was Africans who suffered 360 years of colonialism, 98 years of separate development and 48 years of institutional-ized apartheid. Not only was our land stolen ... our culture was stolen, our language was stolen, our morals and ways of doing things was stolen. We were told that everything black and African was backwards and hidden.[190]

We are a generation into African rule and still a successful and oth-erwise moderate African business leader strikes this harsh anti-colonial tone. A tone that binds influential Africans in common political cause and makes it virtually impossible for multiracial parties like the DA to counter the electoral power of African race solidarity.

You won't hear Bill Gates telling Africans they can either learn Shakespeare or go back to their tribes. That's because he is worried what proud Africans like Professor Bonang Mohale would think about that. Westerners don't have the confidence in their civilization that Master Hui Li has in his. We worry that Professor Mohale will call us a racist for suggesting that he does not have his own civilization and that his best bet is to fall in with ours.

Unlike the Chinese, Africans do not have a 2,500-year legacy of

188. (*Tribe* magazine, Muna Ndlovu, 2022)
189. (*Lean on Me*, 1989)
190. (*Tribe* magazine, Muna Ndlovu, 2022)

state-building, and they don't have a rich history of great religions to underpin those state-building efforts. You can't build a state unless you have the *high gods* of great religions like Christianity and Buddhism. [191] You cannot build a state on the moral system of pre-literate tribalism.

The *WaBenzi*, as some like to parody our African elite, tend to be more passionate about luxury German cars than about building a viable African civilization. Our political elite sold off the state to buy these vehicles. And some still feel the dignity deficit. That's because dignity does not come from expensive cars; it comes from engagement in a meaningful profession. This door is not open to everyone, in which case we must find our dignity in religion and community, in studying the Bible and other sacred texts for the meaning they give to our lonely strivings.

These ideas are considered old-fashioned to progressives, so they've created an ideology that confers racial pride by fiat.

Obioma is right. Only when African countries transform themselves into mining and industrial powers will they overcome the dignity problem. But it will take enormous psychological and cultural sacrifice for an African country to bootstrap itself into socioeconomic relevance. Majority rule is not always the best way to get there. As Rwanda proves. It was a failing state under the previous majority Hutu regime; now under the Tutsis, it is Africa's shining example of economic growth. It took a genocide and overwhelming global sympathy for Paul Kagame's Tutsi rebels for him to enjoy the legitimacy that allows a minority to rule over a majority.

But Rwanda is not like apartheid South Africa. There is no explicit exclusion of Hutus from national political power. Kagame's presidency—rather his tyranny—is the glue that helps his people overcome

---

191. Haidt uses the term *high gods* to reference religions that emerged in the Holocene Age (from 12,000 years ago).

their tribal problems and build a viable state.

That was the hope for South Africa, that Mandela—without being a tyrant—would glue the country together. With his multiracial warmth, Mandela was indeed our glue. It worked for a few years and could have worked for more had Mandela's multiracial magic become infused in our body politic.

In terms of our everyday interactions, South Africa is now one of the world's most diverse, least racist, places. But in the realm of politics, we are as sectarian as ever. In 1994, many from the minorities suspended their intuitive distrust of African rule and celebrated the founding of a unitary non-racial state. Alas, our intuitions were right all along.

THE ANOMIE OF DIVERSITY AND THE WAR ON INTUITION

Some think it's worth modifying our values for the sake of racial equity. Since the 1960s, progressives have tried to make our European race-culture friendlier to other cultures. Disciplines like post-colonial studies teach that Europe has a debt to pay to the indigenous people of the world. Anticolonial scholarship has culminated in critical race theory, which influences political and corporate decision-making with terms like *affirmation, empowerment, transformation, diversity, multiculturalism, social justice*, and *equity*.

These terms are stock in trade for our global intellectual elite and their globalist cosmopolitan ideals. We see the ideals they point to in Angela Merkel's Germany, where foreigners were treated very differently than in the 1940s. Once, the German state annihilated law-abiding citizens who spoke their language, shared their values, and called themselves *German*.

Today, Germans will berate themselves for not being kind enough to refugees. This was famously evidenced by Merkel's about-turn when confronted by a crying Palestinian girl on live television, complaining about her outcast status as a refugee facing deportation: "It is really very unpleasant to look on at how others can really enjoy life while oneself cannot enjoy it."[192] A million Middle Eastern refugees and economic immigrants were the fortunate recipients of Merkel's change of heart, before Germany raised the drawbridge again. People of Middle Eastern provenance once fled Germany on pain of death; today they flee *to* Germany.

In America and Europe today it's not what you think about *greedy rich bosses* or *oppressed workers* that reveals your political sentiments; it's what you think about people who don't speak like you or look like you. Donald Trump intuited that the urban elite had left the white masses behind on the scratchy issue of difference. He played to those who feared immigrants, Muslims, and offshore factories, promising to build a wall around the insiders to keep the outsiders out. Liberals and progressives loathe Trump for his isolationist stance: *Since when do whites have the right to wall themselves off from others?*

If the progressives are right and integration and diversity are unalloyed goods, then why are so few committed to the project? I came across a scholar by the name of Phila Msimang, who cites a "growing body of evidence" that shows "the pervasiveness and persistence of racial thinking in the literature, mainly from studies of history and evolutionary psychology."[193] These studies suggest, "race may be with us far into the future" and "a non-racial society without the recognition of races [may be] out of reach."[194]

This approach coincides with common sense. No society has successfully abolished race. Regardless of the biological significance or otherwise of group difference, it continues to influence—in general terms—who we associate with and share beliefs with, and is likely to do so for generations to come. If humans are wired to recognize racial

---

192. (BBC, 2015)
193. (Msimang, 2018)
194. (Msimang, 2018)

difference and embed it in their behaviour, then no humanist intervention to eliminate racism will succeed.

This is not the standard line promoted by influential cosmopolitan elites, those who control major publications, popular entertainment and the academy—those who promote the ideology of diversity but do not themselves practice it. Like the rest of us, they prefer to associate with people who look like them and think like them.

Why is there such a gap in what we tell ourselves about the world and how we behave?

Jonathan Haidt's landmark works *The Happiness Hypothesis* (2006) and *The Righteous Mind* (2012) contain a startling new theory in the field of social science. The theory says that the intuitive-emotional side of our character guides our behaviors and moral choices. Haidt calls this aspect of us, *the elephant*. Meanwhile, our rational side, *the rider* sitting atop the elephant, plays catchup by providing post-facto commentary.

According to Haidt, the rider is like the president's press secretary, making up stories on the fly to justify the president's decisions.

Before people like Haidt changed the field of moral psychology it was assumed that we were moral creatures by reason and not by intuition … *C'mon! Be reasonable!* But the evidence overwhelmingly supports the unsettling notion that it's the other way round. We make our moral decisions much like our romantic ones—intuitively. The story about why it was such a righteous decision comes after the decision has been made.

No matter what our liberal riders tell us, we're generally not that good at diversity. Ordinary folk have become demoralized at having to pretend to an enthusiasm they don't have—one that was foisted on them by a hypocritical elite.

In *Bowling Alone: The Collapse and Revival of American*

Community (2000), Robert Putnam's research shows that, "ethnic diversity causes a reduction in social capital." As he puts it, "People in ethnically diverse settings seem to hunker down, to pull in like a turtle."[195] In South Africa, they hunker down or head for Perth.

Once upon a time, conflict and difference strengthened in-group ties as tribes resisted outside threats. But today in our anonymous cosmopolitan societies, as Putnam reports, "Diversity seems to trigger not in-group versus out-group division but anomie, or social isolation."[196] This is exactly what has happened in South Africa. There is no ethnic backlash against the tide of diversity. Whites are not planning a breakaway country; they're seeping off to live in places run by people of the same race.

Why has the European race-culture got itself into such a muddle about race and cultural difference? The West used to be defined—to a large degree—by race. You could not separate Western values from the stock of European people who routinely espoused those values around the world. Not anymore. Japan, South Korea, and Singapore also follow Western values and Western-style political systems. From the 1950s on, Western countries became interested in Eastern thought—Buddhism from Tibet and Southeast Asia and feudal Brahminism from India. Then from the 60s, the Civil Rights Movement helped to mainstream African American culture into American life.

Perhaps because of the Holocaust, racism started to become a taboo in America and Europe in the 1950s, accelerating efforts at economic and social integration.

What if the current process of integration continues? Will the European race-culture eventually morph into a multiracial culture, a true *human-culture* that includes all races?

---

195. (Putnam, 2000)
196. (Putnam, 2000)

In some ways this has already happened. Other race-cultures have copied European institutions and found them to their liking. The professionally aspirant from all race-cultures find happiness and success in European race-culture societies, be they America, Europe, or Australia.

There is an abiding exception that confounds. It's partly to do with the worldwide indignity of the black race and the guilt projected onto the European race-culture as the supposed cause for this indignity.

The failure of political integration in South Africa and the general underperformance of African-origin people in the world economy is the great shame whose name dare not be spoken. The progressive framework for interpreting this problem is distorted. It doubles down on blaming whites for being racist. In their iron-clad commitment not to blame the *victim*, progressives turn Africans into children and then turn their brand of anti-racism into a Godly act. This is wrong. European civilization is not only good for Europeans; it has also proved edifying for non-Europeans.

From about the time the English were settling the Eastern Cape (1820s), freed slaves from America and the Caribbean began to settle Liberia. In 1847, they declared themselves the *Republic of Liberia* and drafted a constitution based on the American one. This was Africa's first republic, predating South Africa's Union by sixty-three years.[197]

As a colony run by black American and Caribbean settlers, Liberia enjoyed close ties with America and was championed by liberals in that country. The True Whig Party, a vehicle for Americo-Liberian rule, governed from 1848 to 1980. The Americo-Liberians were black colonists, repatriated ex-slaves who set themselves up as a political elite and bossed about the indigenous tribes, of which there were seventeen.

But it wasn't all bad. Under President William Tubman's rule (1944–1971) Liberia achieved some economic success. It courted

197. Excluding the early Boer republics, which predate Liberia.

Western powers, attracted foreign investment, and diversified the economy away from its dependence on rubber. Tubman died of natural causes and was replaced by William Tolbert, the last Americo-Liberian ruler. Tolbert spoke Kpelle (an indigenous tongue) and had a feel for indigenous grievances. He wanted to give them more representation in government, something conservative Americo-Liberians parodied as *letting the peasants into the kitchen.*[198]

Tolbert was exemplary in many respects, clamping down on corruption, tightening tax collection on foreign companies, and insisting they employ more Liberians. He even instituted a term limit on the presidency, stating, "I will serve my country as long as I have life. I do not have to be president to do so." In 1979, Liberia hosted the Organisation of African Union, where Tolbert was elected its president. This was part of his attempt to reposition Liberia as a proudly African country and not a vassal of America. His improved relations with neighbors also led to the founding of the Economic Community of West African States (ECOWAS).

What could go wrong? By any reasonable estimate, Tolbert was doing everything he could to improve Liberia's relationship with its African neighbors and open the country to foreign investment.

What started off as peaceful demonstrations against a hike in the price of rice led to the *Rice Riots* of 1979. (Tolbert and some of his allies had been implicated in artificially driving up the rice price for personal gain.) Unemployed urban youth (*back street boys*) used the demonstrations as cover to loot and wreak havoc in the capital city of Monrovia.

With internal strife and a depressed rubber market, Liberia's rulers found themselves under pressure but still very much in charge. They

---

198. I found this on Wikipedia, which offers no reference to this quotation in an otherwise well-referenced account of Tolbert.

could at least comfort themselves that the world was on their side. Tolbert was probably about as internationally acceptable as it was possible to be. He enjoyed good diplomatic relations with the Capitalist West and the Communist East, as well as with his African neighbors. President Jimmy Carter visited him in 1978 and did not seem to mind too much that Tolbert was shifting Liberia to a more non-aligned stance in foreign affairs. From a diplomatic perspective, Liberia was enjoying the best of all worlds.

The demise of Tolbert on 12 April 1980 and the ensuing Liberian crisis came as a shock. History tells us that Master Sergeant Samuel Doe and seventeen of his men entered the presidential palace and killed Tolbert, along with twenty-six other high-ranking officials. Ten days later, the head of the True Whig Party was severed when thirteen members of the cabinet were tried by a kangaroo court and executed on a Monrovian beach. Although Doe and his conspirators were indigenous Africans, the coup was not explicitly sold as an overthrow of Americo-Liberian rule. And yet there was celebration in Liberia as indigenous people felt the shackles of colonial rule finally lifted. It didn't make too much difference that these Americo-Liberians were black like them; what mattered was that they felt oppressed by a foreign elite. Indigenous Liberians didn't have a sophisticated critique of the colonists; they were simply tired of being manipulated by people they saw as foreign.

Whatever difficulties Liberians faced under the True Whig Party were small potatoes in comparison to what was to come. Like those early ANC founders, Tolbert and his predecessor William Tubman were eager to avoid the evils of sectarianism. They saw themselves as a bulwark of Enlightenment values; ethnic war was unthinkable.

With Samuel Doe in power, Liberia slid into a morass of tribal conflict. Doe, having achieved power through murder, was illegitimate from the start. He had not declared war against an oppressive minority, or even laid out his grievances against them in writing. He simply marched into the president's palace and murdered Liberia's leaders while they lay sleeping.

What did Africa do on hearing that the recently appointed chairman of the Organisation of African Unity had been murdered in a coup? Besides expressions of shock and outrage, not much. What could they do? Doe was popular with the armed forces, who were also men of indigenous origin. Anyone trying to unseat Doe would have to go to war against Liberia. Because of the subtext of the coup—indigenous people overthrowing colonists—opposing Doe could be construed as reactionary. So, no one did anything and Doe was soon recognised by the OAU, becoming established as the legitimate ruler of Liberia. How had decades of relatively enlightened rule in Liberia been so easily revoked? What happened after Tolbert's murder makes this question worth answering.

From 1980, Liberia struggled to resolve its ethnic tensions, with warring parties organised along tribal lines. An estimated 250,000 people, in a population of only five million, were killed in civil wars that saw Doe assassinated in 1990 and Charles Taylor come to power in 1997 before his murderous reign finally ended in 2003. Throughout the chaos, Liberia's economy shrank by 90 per cent.

The Liberian story has a parallel in a country to the south: Rhodesia. Liberia and Rhodesia—two small African countries founded and ruled by colonial minorities whom the world abandoned in 1980 to indigenous rebel forces.

While Liberia's transition was by coup, Rhodesia's was by guerrilla war, followed by negotiated settlement and credible elections. In both countries, the colonial minority helped keep tribalism in check, and in both ordinary folks were significantly worse off for indigenization.

In 1980, a democratic election delivered Mugabe to power in Zimbabwe, ending a civil war that had lasted fifteen years and in which the two African liberation groups, ZANU (Shona) and ZAPU (Matabele), fought a classic peasant revolution. They framed their struggle not in terms of civil rights but in terms of anti-colonialism, calling it the Second Chimurenga. In the First Chimurenga (1896–1897), British imperialist Cecil John Rhodes (through his British South African Company), put down a rebellion by the Matabele and the Shona in what is now Zimbabwe. The rebellion was interesting for two reasons. 1) It involved a collaborative attack on Europeans by the two main African ethnic groups; 2). It was inspired by African religious leaders. One of the main leaders, Sekuru Kaguvi, claimed to channel *Mwari*, the Shona God.

By calling their liberation struggle the *Second Chimurenga*, ZANU and ZAPU were implying that Africans had a sacred ancestral duty to rid the country of whites. How is it that Europeans won the First Chimurenga in Zimbabwe but lost the second? What had demoralized their efforts at nation-building along Western lines that they conceded to ZANU, a party unfit to govern a modern country? When colonial forces crushed the uprising in 1897 and killed the spirit mediums who inspired it, the news was celebrated in Britain. This was in stark contrast to how the Second Chimurenga ended.

By 1979, whites, led by Ian Smith and his Rhodesian Front Party, had come to a settlement with moderate Africans. The country had an African prime minister and president, while the civil service, judiciary, military, and police remained in white hands, as did a third of parliamentary seats. Such has been the murderous disaster of ZANU's rule, many Zimbabweans may look back on 1979 with a sense of nostalgia.[199]

---

199. Noting that the 1980 agreement guaranteed whites 20% of parliamentary seats; this was withdrawn by ZANU in 1987.

The conservative Margaret Thatcher, British prime minister at the time, conceded to pressure from the Commonwealth and to the African nationalists, who rejected Smith's power-sharing solution. In 1980, all parties submitted to a new democratic process, this time majoritarian, and ZANU proved that it did indeed enjoy widespread support, winning 63 per cent of the vote.[200] But people had voted along tribal lines, Matabele for ZAPU and Shona for ZANU; Zimbabwe became a country run by a tribe. Mugabe duly fulfilled the racist white prophecy of African post-colonial states—*one man, one vote, once*—eventually turning the country into a de facto one-party state, in contravention of the agreement that handed him power in the first place.[201]

Was Mugabe a tribalist who believed it his sacred right to run the country like a chief, as if *Mwari* the great creator had bequeathed it to him? Mugabe may have been a political tribalist, but he was certainly not an African tribalist. He was, if anything, an Anglophile, keen for the children of the country to be educated in the British tradition.

What went wrong? Zimbabwe's transition happened at the height of the Cold War. ZANU and ZAPU received support from China and the Soviet Union. When applied to Zimbabwe, the Marxist narrative of oppressed versus oppressor made for a clear moral case. The West claimed the moral high ground over the Communist East on the basis that they supported democracy and self-determination. They therefore could not reasonably hold back the aspiration of African nationalists, who were willing to lay down arms in exchange for an election.

It would seem on the surface that what sank Zimbabwe was racism. Whites were sufficiently racist—with exceptions—to resist integration

---

200. Notwithstanding allegations of voter intimidation.
201. Zimbabwe did not officially become a one-party state and faced serious opposition from the MDC, who probably won the 2008 elections. The results were massaged, and observers were intimidated; the upshot was that the AU pressured the parties to enter a GNU (government of national unity). But ZANU-PF remain firmly entrenched in power to this day despite their failings.

and set themselves apart as a special class. After defeating the Matabele and Shona in 1897, they needed to nurture unity and reconciliation. Instead, they set themselves up in colonial splendour, complete with teams of loyal servants and ample good land. They did not marry the locals or create a strong African petit bourgeois to whom they could entrust the country. It was too easy for the African nationalists to revive old colonial hurts, aggravated with vengeful Marxist rhetoric. In 1965, white Rhodesians should have chosen a moderate, long-term approach to their situation. And they should have stayed close to the mothership: Britain. They chose instead Ian Smith for prime minister, whose response to British *meddling* in Rhodesia's affairs was UDI—a Unilateral Declaration of Independence. That move was as stupid as apartheid, making it that much harder for friends in Europe to lend a helping hand to their beleaguered white cousins in Africa.

But this interpretation of the failings of white Rhodesia is simply a rehashing of the old trope: *whites are so irremediably racist that they can't possibly make peace in a proud African state.* And it does not account for the Liberian story, which wasn't about race and yet still ended up like Zimbabwe: a ruinous indigenous takeover.

In 2005, Mugabe instituted Operation Murambatsvina (*move the rubbish*), bulldozing shacks and makeshift homes of hundreds of thousands of people who had migrated to urban centres after the rural economy collapsed in the wake of his confiscation of white farmland. With his attacks on gays, colonialism, and Britain, Mugabe delighted in playing the race card. And he used it again to defend the madness of Murambatsvina. But the country and the card were given to him by the West.[202]

---

202. Mugabe is also complicit in the Gukurahundi (1982–1987), where 20,000 Ndebele civilians were killed by the Zimbabwe military. The ruling party was officially renamed from ZANU to ZANU-PF after the two anticolonial forces (ZAPU and ZANU) formed a political accord, helping end the violence.

If facts on the ground count and the lives of ordinary Africans really matter, then the True Whig Party under a moderate like Tolbert should have carried on running Liberia, and white Rhodesians should have retained a measure of control in the new country of Zimbabwe.

Tolbert was not perfect, but by Africa's low standards of governance he was doing a decent job of reforming Liberia along liberal lines. He was an educated man who grasped modern ideas of economics and governance. Similarly, Rhodesia's white minority recognised the political imperative of indigenous support to legitimate their rule. Like Tolbert, they were also trying to reform the country along more humane lines. And like Tolbert, they didn't believe in race war.

In a saner world, Liberia and Rhodesia would have stayed satellites of America and Britain. The prevailing sociopolitical narrative in the English-speaking world offered little succor to white Rhodesians and Americo-Liberians. It offers them even less today.

In the past, civilizations lost wars against marauding tribes: the Mongols overran China, and Germanic tribes terrorized the city-states of fifth-century Europe. Back then civilization was tangible, with buildings, libraries, roads, and aqueducts. If your books were burning and your temples were being desecrated, you knew your civilization was in trouble. Today, civilization is virtual, a set of ideas and values that holds society together. In the twentieth century, the Anglo-American virtual civilization surrendered itself, not to hordes of warriors, but to an idea: the idea that it had no right to interfere in political indigenization, no matter how ruinous the process.

To be fair, it's very hard for westerners to know what to do when African countries are beset by political crises. As the example of Biafra shows.

If you want to eat the frog of African failure, then Nigeria is a good toad to start with. It's hard not to fall into exaggeration when describing the country's woes. A friend who is in the business of writing about African security put it to me this way: "When the large-scale capture and enslavement of schoolgirls in parts of your country is now so common as not to be considered newsworthy, you know you're screwed!"

What went wrong in Africa's most populous country? In 1960, Britain granted Nigeria independence. They had ruled the place in the same way that Verwoerd was hoping to rule black South Africa, through fiefdoms run by local chiefs. They did a tolerably good job of this, as Nigeria's famous author Chinua Achebe attests:

> Here is a piece of heresy: the British governed their colony of Nigeria with considerable care. There was a very highly competent cadre of government officials imbued with a high level of knowledge of how to run a country ... The British had the experience of governing and doing it competently. I am not justifying colonialism. But it is important to face the fact that British colonies, more or less, were expertly run.

Britain had something that Nigeria could not emulate; it had a coherent race-culture that could produce a class of competent, loyal civil servants, dedicated to King and Country. Nigeria did not have that, so in 1966 it started to come apart at the seams. At first, ethnicity wasn't really an issue; the Africanist spirit had animated the postcolonial independence movement, there was a real commitment to overcome the ethnicity trap.

But coups and countercoups in 1966 led to a pogrom against the Igbos. In revenge for the coup that killed the popular Sir Ahmadu Bello, tens of thousands of Igbos were massacred in the north. Over a million Igbos fled back to their traditional homeland in the south-east and declared it a republic in May 1967—the Republic of Biafra.

Who were the Igbos and why are they important to this story? The Igbos are like the Tutsi of Rwanda: a petit-bourgeois in the colonial era who have a decent shot at nation-building in the postcolonial era. According to Chinua Achebe, they are part-tribe and part-nation—like the Jews before 1948.[203]

As Achebe notes, "With unparalleled rapidity, the Igbos advanced fastest in the shortest period of time of all Nigeria's ethnic groups. Like the Jews, to whom they have frequently been likened, they progressed despite being a minority in the country, filling the ranks of the nation's educated, prosperous upper classes."[204]

Today, the oil-rich south-eastern Nigeria is populated mainly by Igbos, who constitute about thirty million of the total Nigerian population of 211 million. For three years in the late '60s, this part of Nigeria became its own country, attracting excitement from quarters in the West, who saw it as the seed of a unique African flowering.

In 1899, Britain had blundered into a war against the nation-building efforts of the Boers. In 1967, under Harold Wilson's Labour Party, it blundered into supporting, along with the Soviets, the Nigerian federal forces against the Biafrans. Why? Because Britain's leaders rejected the idea that this nascent country, which included 35 per cent non-Igbos, was being built on pride in Igbo ethnicity.

The Biafrans were led by their founding (and only ever) president, Odumegwu Ojukwu, then the Eastern Region's military governor. Ojukwu seemed to have been out of touch with the suffering of his people, holding on for an unlikely victory while they starved. When the end came in January 1970, he fled to President Félix Houphouët-Boigny's Ivory Coast for protection. Ojukwu was later pardoned by Nigeria, returning in 1982 and unsuccessfully running for president,

203. The point is made in a Wikipedia entry that references it, with a quotation, from (Achebe, 2000).
204. (Achebe, 2012)

before dying in the UK in 2011. Nigeria honoured him with a full military funeral.

By some accounts, when the war started, Biafra had no firearms and no modern military gear—only knives and cutlasses. This is according to Felix Nwankwo Oragwu, who spearheaded Biafra's Research and Production group (RAP), a team of scientists who developed weapons for the secessionists. Their *ogbunigwe* was a rocket launcher of some effect, which you can read about in Oragwu's 2010 book *Scientific and Technological Innovations in Biafra: (The "Ogbunigwe" Fame 1967–1970)*.

Biafra was not quite as technologically super-advanced as Wakanda, but Biafrans were proud of their self-reliance and their homegrown scientific achievements. In a BBC article from 2020, "Remembering Nigeria's Biafra War That Many Prefer to Forget," Oragwu, who continued his work as a scientist and educator in Nigeria after the war, strikes a bitter tone. He bemoans the fact that after the war, the Igbos got involved in the game of national politics, instead of building on the technical prowess displayed during the war. "Biafra would have been a technological nation and would have been able to compete with anybody," says Oragwu. "That is what makes me sad. By this time, we would have been competing with at least South Korea."[205]

For Oragwu, the war was not about ethnic chauvinism but about, "the opportunity to … reject the colonial design." Which he explains as: "Nigeria was programmed by the British colonial authorities not to participate in production and manufacture of global technologies." *Echoes of a nascent Wakanda.*

The war and the atrocities committed by a larger, better equipped Nigerian army were something of a cause célèbre; Kurt Vonnegut visited Biafra and came away in such a state of grief that he found himself

---

205. (Nwaubani, 2020)

"barking like a dog."[206]

It's hard to know what to make of the Biafran War. A minority ethnic group secedes on the grounds of ethnic persecution. A left-wing British government and the Soviet Union back Nigeria in its war against the secessionists. Finally, Biafra is defeated by a blockade after over a million people, mainly children, starve to death.

Achebe cites the British journalist Richard West on the subject: "Biafra is more than a human tragedy. Its defeat, I believe, would mark the end of African independence. Biafra was the first place I had been to in Africa where the Africans themselves were truly in charge."[207]

Why did Britain join in the genocidal suppression of a genuine African self-determination movement? We must rewind our story to the Berlin Conference of 1884–85 to answer that one.

The Berlin Conference included all important nations of the European race-culture, who set the political boundaries under which Africans live to this day. No Africans were present at the meeting. The Berlin Conference was a cartoonish example of European colonial culpability. The conference set the tone for the *scramble for Africa*, where European powers, mostly out of geopolitical rivalry with each other, carved up the continent to their pleasure. The most heinous upshot of the conference was that King Leopold of Belgium (1835–1909) would continue to extract rubber from the Congo at the cost of millions of African lives. In 1876, Leopold set up the International Association for the Exploration and Civilization of Central Africa (later renamed the International Association of the Congo). The writer Joseph Conrad parodied it as the *International Society for the Suppression of Savage Customs*.

Leopold extracted ivory and rubber from the Congo at a horrible

---

206. (Achebe, 2012)
207. (Achebe, 2012, p. 72)

cost. Historians cannot agree on the figure, and estimates range wildly: from one to fifteen million Congolese killed by the trade. In 1890, Conrad worked on a river steamboat for a Belgian trading company. Taking the wheel from an ill skipper, he guided the boat to Kindu, in the heart of the Congo. Some ten years later he weaved those experiences into *Heart of Darkness*.

In the novel, Charles Marlow journeys into the interior to track down Kurtz, an ivory trader who has *gone native*. [208] Conrad depicts Europe's involvement in Africa in an unflattering light, suggesting that the real heart of darkness lies not in the African forest but in the souls of European adventurers and their backers. Perhaps European civilization harbors a dark secret?

By the standards of the day, *Heart of Darkness* (1899) is anti-racist and anti-imperialist. Conrad muses that perhaps colonialism is simply an excuse to take land "away from those who have a different complexion or slightly flatter noses than ourselves."[209] It is not hard to connect Conrad's disquiet about colonial plunder with the current ideological fashion of cultural relativism. Of Polish heritage, Conrad modelled himself after an English gentleman and believed in European values—but not by way of blind faith.[210] His writing evidences a man wrestling monsters—inner ones. *Heart of Darkness* is somewhat insular, it does not share in the world of the indigenous character. Africans are depicted as mere props in a European drama—like those Africans I cried over in *Tarzan*.

Not only does *Heart of Darkness* anticipate Jung, it anticipates what Jung anticipated—Europe's descent into savagery during World

---

208. Conrad preceded *Heart of Darkness* with a story along similar lines to the novella, *An Outpost of Progress*.
209. (Denby, 1995) Quotation sourced from the Denby article.
210. He was actually born in what is today Ukraine, Berdychiv, which was known as a Jewish town, then under the rule of Tzarist Russia.

War II. Francis Ford Coppola's era-defining *Apocalypse Now* (1979) is loosely based on the novel, and turns Conrad's moral tale into a psychological drama set during the Vietnam War.

Kurtz, the *supreme representative* of European civilization is the ghostly figure that Marlowe, the protagonist, pursues. Although, *all Europe has gone into making him*, Kurtz lives in a jungle compound as a self-styled chief among the natives, *an emissary of pity and science and progress, and devil knows what else.* Kurtz is sleeping with local lasses and putting his enemies' heads on poles.

Conrad's tale is a psychological thriller, a journey into Jung's shadow, into Freud's Id. David Denby writes of Conrad:

> Here was the last great Victorian, insisting on responsibility and order, and fighting, at the same time, an exhausting and often excruciating struggle against uncertainty and doubt of every kind, such that he cast every truth in his fictions as a mocking illusion and turned his morally didactic tale into an endlessly provocative and dismaying battle between stoical assumption of duty and perverse complicity in evil.[211]

If you live in South Africa and you aspire to being liberal and civilized, then you will find yourself similarly engaged in existential *battle between stoical assumption of duty and perverse complicity in evil.*

For Chinua Achebe, though, Conrad had not battled hard enough. In a famous 1975 essay, the otherwise reasonable Achebe called Joseph Conrad "a bloody racist," saying that Conrad "projects the image of Africa as 'the other world,' the antithesis of Europe and therefore of civilization, a place where man's vaunted intelligence and refinement are finally mocked by triumphant bestiality."[212]

According to Achebe, Europeans simply cannot help themselves.

211. (Denby, 1995)
212. (Achebe, 1975)

Even our well-meaning attempts to understand other, serve only to reify our position as a racially exclusive civilization. According to Achebe, "white racism against Africa is such a normal way of thinking that its manifestations go completely undetected." Perhaps Achebe has cause to lash out against our lazy European assumptions, which—it could be argued—led to Britain's culpability in "the ruining of a rare and genuine national culture at the moment of its birth."[213]

Was Biafra a Wakanda in the making, a home-grown African civilization finding its feet as a nation-state? Biafra goes by another name: *Igbo Land*. If it ever became a nation-state, it would have been one mainly defined by shared ethnic identity. Before the 1960s, it was conventional wisdom that *shared ethnic identity* is a good starting point for nation-building. Nothing has changed. It's still the best foundation for nation-building but we're not allowed to say that because progressive elites would rather we drank their diversity Kool-Aid.

The Fengu, the Igbo, and the Wakandans represent, in strange ways, a mythical African nation-state: indigenous peoples on a civilizing mission of their own.

Biafra was a potential African success story. With the built-in trust networks that come with shared ethnicity and culture, the Igbos were solving those hard problems of turning tribe into state. Like the Fengu, under European rule they advanced, leveraging the opportunities offered by Enlightenment values.

Biafra exposed the great lie in progressive thought—that there is no such thing as human nature. This is the lie that contributed to Harold Wilson's complicity in genocide and the destruction of one of Africa's most promising efforts at nation-building.

The fact is that politicized Africans do not seem to want a

---

213. (Achebe, 2012) This quote is from Stanley Diamond, with whom Achebe clearly agrees on the matter.

readymade foreign civilization to which they must adapt. They want to evolve their own civilization from wherever they find themselves. For all his criticisms of Nigeria's governance, Achebe holds out on the dream of a home-grown civilization. He tells us: "The very existence of this alphabet [Nsibidi, invented by the west African Ekoi people in the 1700s] without any Latin or Arabic antecedent, is a rebuke to all those who have claimed over the centuries that Africa has no history, no writing, and no civilization!"[214]

Joe Clark, Professor Bonang Mohale, the people who made Wakanda, and even Chinua Achebe, all seem bent on the idea that Africans, or African Americans for that matter, have their own civilization worth building on from the ground up. Would Achebe, were he alive today, call for Britain to redeem its historical sin by wholeheartedly supporting the cause of Biafra? Would he ask them to do for Biafra what they're doing for Ukraine?

In a time of historical twists, can we expect one here in South Africa, with minorities in the Western Cape collaborating to form a breakaway country on the grounds of security concerns? Achebe tells us that, "the only valid basis for existence is one that gives security to you and your people. It is as simple as that."[215] Our cities are badly decayed, lawlessness lurks, abetted by a corrupt civil service. The security we have as minorities is not delivered by the state but paid for and organised privately. We have grounds to break away from this failing state.

In 1994, white South Africa surrendered its security for the pale guarantees of a constitution. Our state is meant to dignify the constitution by embodying its spirit of patriotism and socioeconomic justice. Thus far, African majority rule has degraded these values. How?

---

214. (Achebe, 2012, p. 192)
215. (Achebe, 2012, p. 71)

As Justice Potter Stewart wrote in a 1964 judgement on obscenity in film: "I shall not attempt to define the kinds of material I understand to be embraced within that shorthand description 'hard-core pornography'. But I know it when I see it."[216] How do we know when enough is enough and our order has been sufficiently degraded for us to give up on its credibility? The mediocrity of African majority rule in South Africa is akin to the mediocrity displayed by African majority rule in Nigeria, on which Achebe comments: "Mediocrity destroys the very fabric of a country as surely as a war—ushering in all sorts of banality, ineptitude, corruption, and debauchery ... That, in my humble opinion, is precisely where Nigeria finds itself today."[217] It's also where South Africa finds itself in 2022. My rant about civilization is simply a cry for us to overcome the grinding mediocrity of African rule.

Achebe lived out his later years in the US. I assume he would put up with some level of mediocrity in Nigeria. But Achebe lost hope in Nigeria because the country devolved back into tribalism and is nowhere close to being on the path of political order. The example of Nigeria, and that of other post-colonial African states haunts South Africa—we are civilization's stepchild.

216. (Stewart, 2012)
217. (Achebe, 2012, p. 236)

NO CIVILIZATION WITHOUT POLITICAL ORDER, AND VICE VERSA

I n his landmark *The Origins of Political Order* (2012), Francis Fukuyama tells us there are three pillars to political order: state-building, accountable government, and rule of law. The abiding example of state-building is China, which has been engaged in the project for some 2,500 years; the abiding example of accountable government and rule of law is the West. China and the West represent two successful models of political development.

Even though our 1994 transition was meant to deliver accountable government and shore up the legitimacy of our legal system, it has offered mixed results in terms of overall political development. Under Mandela and Mbeki, things were not too bad. Mbeki was flawed, but at least he had a vision for a solid black state within a pan-African context. By contrast, Zuma was thoroughly tribal, selling off bits of the state to keep friends and family sweet, and degrading parliamentary decorum with his uncontrolled fits of laughter. Mbeki centralised power while Zuma exchanged state power for loyalty from regional party bosses like Ace Magashule and David Mabuza.

What if an African ruler and his clique were sincere about African state-building but lacked the necessary bureaucratic personnel? The Ottoman Empire came up with a curious solution for such a problem. They captured Balkan children and forced them to become slave-warriors and slave-bureaucrats—*Janissaries* as they were called. Janissaries were educated slaves loyal to the Sultan. The Sultan could not trust his own people to put state before tribe, so he stole blond boys from Bulgaria to do his imperial soldiering and administering.[218]

South Africa is still heavily reliant on its *Janissaries*: white and Indian expertise. Our African rulers are caught in a bind. They need their Janissary class to help them deliver on the aspiration of a solid black state. Yet, they don't want to rely on those who—unlike the Sultan's Janissaries—are ideologically opposed to their political masters.

Today, tribes are a problem because we live in nation-states, which are meant to transcend the sectarian pull of tribe. European colonists did not quite appreciate the subtleties of tribalism. Fukuyama puts it nicely: "A mistake commonly made by European colonialists in India and Africa was assuming that tribal leadership amounted to the same thing as the authority of a local lord in a feudal society, when the two were actually quite different."[219]

In South Africa today, many Africans are sympathetic to the slogan *expropriation* [of land] *without compensation*. Almost everyone from the minorities (including the arch-communist Jeremy Cronin) is against the idea. That's because we're approaching the land problem from the perspective of two completely different political orders. Fukuyama asks, "what drives tribalism?" His answer: "a deep-seated urge to promote and protect the interests of descendants, friends, and clients against the requirements of an impersonal social system."[220]

---

218. Some historical commentators point out that the Ottoman Empire was a predatory state and not particularly interested in true state-building.
219. (Fukuyama, 2012, p. 240)
220. (Fukuyama, 2012, p. 209)

There we have it: Jacob Zuma, Ace Magashule, David Mabuza, and the whole cabal of ANC gangster-politicians are not merely bad-faith actors bent on using politics to accumulate cash. They are driven by a deep-seated urge—something like religious faith—to resist the imposition of an impersonal social system in helping their friends, family, and patronage clients. White South Africans can't deal with it because not only is this worldview removed from our current liberal humanism—it's a step removed from feudalism, the worldview of our medieval ancestors.

Fukuyama parses the distinction between tribal societies and feudal ones: "Once a feudal lord's rights were legally established, they were not subject to constant renegotiation in the way that authority within a lineage [tribe] was. Legal title to property, whether held by the strong or the weak, conveyed a clear power to buy or sell it without restriction imposed by a kin-based social system."[221]

Why do some prominent Africans question the sanctity of the rule of law and of the constitution? Maybe they feel themselves to be interdependent with a community and therefore obliged to sustain the unity of this network of people. This sacred moral obligation may involve *protecting friends, family, and business networks from the interference of an impersonal social system.*

Tribes are all about interdependence and sustaining cohesion. True tribal leaders are not tyrannical, like Shaka, they are communal and consensus-seeking.[222] Zulu *nationhood* is an interesting exception in South Africa. It is not so much that Shaka's legacy has made the Zulus warlike and inclined to ethnic posturing. This may be true, but it's overstated. The more important fact is that *amaZulu* are the country's biggest ethnolinguistic group; and therefore in a better position to play the tribal game.

---

221. (Fukuyama, 2012, p. 240)
222. Credo Mutwa, an expert on African mythology, makes this point about Shaka, see *Indaba, My Children*.

But we must not judge them for that. Tribalism is the natural state, both psychologically and politically, as Fukuyama tells us, "Tribes made up of patrons and clients linked through reciprocity and personal ties are one of the great constants of political development."[223]

Since Zuma's presidency, the ANC has split into two factions. In today's political language we could frame it as *social democrats versus hard Africanists*. The few from the minorities still in the ANC are social democrats dedicated to state-building and to better living conditions for the poor. [224] They're at odds with the hard Africanists in the ANC and EFF, whom I typify as *politically tribal* and who are inclined to trump the social democrats with the dreaded indigenous race card.

Kinship groups and clannish alliances confound the ANC's aspiration of a solid black state. Hard Africanists have no qualms with devolving the state to local rent seekers. As of writing, the social democratic Ramaphosa is at the helm and the center holds. That does not mean the rent-seeking ends. Politicians are less likely to hand out paper bags of money as they did in the Zuma years. But patronage continues in the form of protected state employment, state-business patronage networks, and rents in the form of preferential ownership.[225]

Political tribalism is a headache for social democrats—for those who care about building a capable developmental state. The powerful kinship actors are not too worried about a capable state because they do not believe in abstract ideals like poverty reduction. They don't lie awake at night worrying that South Africa is not Sweden.

How do we respond to a ruling party that we acknowledge as being legitimately elected, but which harbors tribal factions dedicated to looting and even sabotaging the state? Do we as the professional-managerial class self-fulfil the prophecy of a failed state or do we

223. (Fukuyama, 2012, p. 78) slight paraphrasing
224. The somewhat deranged Carl Niehaus is the only exception I can think of.
225. As previously attributed to Mcebisi Jonas.

endorse the Africanist project by serving it as loyal Janissaries? What is the nature of our interdependence to the state? Is there a moral foundation by which the middle-class in this country can make sense of the place?

Indian feudal ethics suggests an answer. With no tyranny, limited legal frameworks, and limited repression, Indians developed a functional political order. The trick behind it was that the Brahmins, the priesthood, were the highest class.[226] They were above the clerks and warriors (*Kshatriyas*) and above the merchants and artisans (*Vaishyas*). Untouchables were like a shadow class, lurking outside of the system. With the Brahmins at the top, this feudal order was dignified by the embrace of a sophisticated religious cosmology, the sort of civilizational balm America needs to heal from its culture wars.

Modern western countries cannot resort to tyranny, as China does. They need a priesthood like feudal India had, to dignify the project of state-building. We in the professional-managerial class are that priesthood.

Unlike the original Brahminic class our modern priestly class is multiracial.[227] The doors of professionalism, technical achievement, and managerial excellence are open to all races. You see that in South Africa today, with Indians overcoming white racism and excelling in the professions; black Africans who are competent professionals also find success here, as they do in Western countries.

What defines a healthy modern society? It is one in which the professions are trusted and where good professionals thrive. The political game to turn management and the professions into a site of anti-racist struggle will end in catastrophe. No country can achieve modern industrial status without a sufficiently meritocratic society to encourage the

226. This is a rendering of a point made by Fukuyama.
227. Disconcertingly, *Varna* (the name for the system) means *color*, and indeed tribal people and untouchables were excluded from it.

growth of the professional-managerial class. African countries remain poor and backward because they cannot muster the requisite depth of professional-managerial talent to run an efficient society that guarantees opportunity for its people.

To sum up the clash from the perspective of my priesthood: *We in the professional-managerial priesthood have a sacred duty to build a modern industrial economy with high rates of employment; the African political elite who run the country have a sacred tribal duty to share in state resources and support their circle of friends, family, and business networks.*

The constitution, flawed as it is, dedicates us to the promotion of human flourishing and sacred individual expression. Therefore, we in the professional-managerial priesthood are the inheritors of this state.

When Mandela came to power in 1994, he embodied our constitutional values and drew on the talents of those from the minorities to help build an inclusive country. With his charm and warmth, the Mandela *magic* encouraged a spirit of interdependence as per Shweder's "feudal ethics" with its "vision of allegiance and asymmetrical reciprocity."[228] But feudal ethics were never institutionalized here. Instead we followed the American model whereby, as Shweder tells us, hierarchy is often associated with "tyranny, exploitation, and overreaching entitlement."[229]

Feudal societies solve the hierarchy problem by giving people a special role within the Great Chain of Being, which wasn't very woke, but at least you knew where you stood. What do we replace it with? With what does modern ideology substitute the social glue of feudal interdependence?

Political orders need hierarchies. South Africa's race hierarchy has

228. (Shweder, et al., 1997)
229. (Shweder, et al., 1997)

been replaced by a blunt racial majoritarianism which now threatens ruin.

Alas, we live in times where it is better to be ruinous than racist.

BOSMAN, BECK, WILBER, AND THE DEVELOPMENTAL STATE

At my high school we had a teacher called *Pekie* Hall. His real name was Robin Hall, but the boys called him *Pekie* as an ironic joke about his notoriously racist ideology. *Pekie*, a demeaning term for Africans, is a corruption of *umpheki*, which is *isiZulu* for cook, a reference to the *good old African cook boy*, the caricatured smiling Zulu man in his wash-boy uniform.

Hall was a British Israelite, a strange bunch who say that Brits, not Jews, are the descendants of the lost tribes of Israel, with Anglo-Saxons atop a racial hierarchy that has Africans at the bottom. In my penultimate year of high school, I found myself acting in an operetta with Mr Hall: Gilbert and Sullivan's *HMS Pinafore*. It was directed by a science teacher, Mr Thomson, who was the ideological opposite of Hall, having been investigated by the police for alleged communist activity. At one point in the show the male actors do a little jig with the females, taking their hands and giving them a twirl. Every time we had to twirl, Robin Hall found himself paired with a black actress. Every time he changed position to make sure he didn't touch her.[230]

---

230. In the 1980s, private white schools could enroll black pupils.

We all pretended not to notice but it was embarrassing and shameful to witness.

Thankfully, most white South Africans do not fear black skin like that. Still, *we need to talk about Robin*. We need to unload our baggage. And we need to listen when Africans unload their baggage to us.

Some Africans call their baggage a *black tax*. I once sat in the office of the chairman of Eskom, waiting for an interview. This was during those years of State Capture. I was working freelance for *Icawa*, head of employee engagement at Eskom.[231] She and two others were in the room; I was the only non-African and the only non-Eskom employee. The subject turned to corruption and why the new African elite was stealing more than the Afrikaners did. I tried to assure them that their leadership was stealing because of what had happened during apartheid—or some such drivel. Icawa put me right: "No, Angus, it's because we are responsible to our extended families; they pressure us to support them. We are tempted into corruption to look after them."[232]

Francis Fukuyama would be happy to know that his theories are well understood—in practical terms that is—here in South Africa. I was paid by Eskom to provide ideological cover for a ruling elite who were behaving just as Francis Fukuyama said. But I still believed there was sufficient momentum behind the state-building project; that there were enough politicians in the ANC willing to bow to an impersonal social system, even at the expense of alienating friends, family and business networks. I still had some hope when I wrote phrases like, "we will not achieve such an economy without both a strong and capable developmental state and an inclusive, fast-growing private sector. We should not be asked to choose one or the other. We need both." I wrote this for people like President Ramaphosa (from whom I borrowed this

---

231. Not her real name; pronounced *E-tsa-wa*.
232. Words to that effect.

particular phrase of propagandistic banality). After a few years of this sort of thing it began to dawn on me that I was peddling a lie.

In theory, the idea was that up-and-coming African professionals and managers would take the wheel at the state-owned enterprises and direct these vehicles of indigenous redress and economic justice along the road of African self-reliance.

The reality was that many Africans in these organizations were an indulged class who saw themselves as the entitled inheritors of good middle-class jobs, regardless of their expertise and commitment. But someone still has to keep the lights on. The upshot was that outside contractors and consultancies had to be called in to plug the gaping holes caused by affirmative action.

One of those consultancies was McKinsey, which helped Eskom build its two new coal-fired power stations, Medupi and Kusile. Separate to my freelance work for Icawa at Eskom, I worked with a McKinsey team to write a project execution plan for Medupi Power Station, at the time one of the world's biggest infrastructure projects.

I walked around that industrial miracle in the far-northern bush-veld of South Africa, asking engineers and managers about what they were doing and how this project was being implemented.

This was during Zuma's presidency, when the vultures were circling to feed off big contracts. The ANC, through its dubious investment wing Chancellor House, did a deal with Hitachi, funneling large sums of money back to the ruling party and the politically connected.

About midway through the Medupi build, in 2013, Icawa sent me out to cover President Jacob Zuma honoring a construction milestone. He was to press a big red button that was meant to be switching on the electricity.

The red button was turning nothing on; it was a Punch and Judy show for publicity and solidarity. The workers weren't having any of it; they booed Zuma ... not because of State Capture but because of the ANC's interminable factional in-fighting.

The engineers sitting around me assured me that the button was fake; it was all show for the cameras. But speeches had to be made and booing workers had to be heard. Zuma's cunning grin and infamous skirt-chasing were in evidence. There was also an ugly incident. A camerawoman got too close to Zuma's security detail. She was very quickly and thoroughly dominated, without being beaten as such. She shouted in defense but backed away smartly enough.

Brian Dames, Eskom CEO at the time, seemed to be enjoying the fact that *Teflon* Zuma was squirming a little. Dames joked about it in his speech: "Uneasy rests the head that wears the crown."

Brian Dames and Jacob Zuma weren't the real story though, and neither were the dissatisfied workers. The real story was that Medupi and Kusile were being built by a consortium of companies and consultancies from around the world and that these professional-managerial experts would overcome South Africa's governance dysfunction to build two of the world's largest, most advanced coal-fired power stations.

If you want to see the professional-managerial class at its most concentrated and collaborative, visit a large-scale industrial project. Extraordinary people are called to do extraordinary things. Oliver Stone made a film about it—*Platoon* (1986). You're called to a foreign land to overcome mediocrity and spread your Western values—by force if need be. You have little time to reflect on your moral foundations as you engage in *an endlessly provocative and dismaying battle between stoical assumption of duty and perverse complicity in evil.* Do you choose duty or evil; are you going to be *Willem Dafoe* (Sergeant Elias) or *Tom Berenger* (Staff Sergeant Barnes)?

McKinsey employs the elite from the professional-managerial

class; it's their business model. You buy elite talent out of college, identifying conscientious types with low self-esteem, and then you put them in teams and rent them out at a premium.

Eskom paid me to tell its stakeholders a story about a developing state powered by African experts. However, it was minorities and ex-pats doing the developing of the state, with Africans conferring sociopolitical legitimacy on the project and being afforded professional-managerial opportunities.

For those three months that I worked on-site in 2014, we would drive to Medupi from our motel in the local town of Lephalale, passing Matimba Power Station on the way. Matimba is rated at four thousand MW (only 17% less than Medupi) and was built in-house by Eskom to budget and to schedule, with far fewer outside consultants involved. It was completed in only four years (1987–1991) and has worked reliably and should continue to do so to 2040. Like everything else before 1994, Matimba was unapologetically built by white initiative and black labour.

Medupi and Kusile were built in a new era of African self-reliance. Whatever that ideology means, it made these large-scale projects even more complicated. They have run a decade over schedule and billions of dollars over budget and have been plagued by corruption scandals.

Eskom had a formidable fleet of coal-fired power stations before 1994, the very engine room of the only economy in Africa to achieve widespread and widescale industrialization. Under Mbeki, Eskom was neglected; under Zuma, it was plundered. So badly was it plundered that McKinsey refused to make anything from their enormous consultancy commitments. In 2017, they announced they would return the billion rands in consultancy fees earned while the country was experiencing

State Capture. When is it not State Capture?[233]

On announcing a second payback (six hundred million rands) in 2020 for work at other state-owned enterprises, McKinsey posted a *Mea culpa*: "We stand by the value of our work. However, in line with our determination to do what is right and be guided by our firm's earlier commitments to Eskom, we will return fees for projects that—even indirectly—may have been related to State Capture. That is not something our firm is willing to accept."

What is McKinsey willing to accept? Interestingly, the biggest gripe I heard about them was that you couldn't form relationships; no sooner would you start building a productive relationship with a McKinsey consultant and they would be whisked off to another *study* (i.e., job) in another country.

However, McKinsey was aware of the need to build social connection among colleagues, and so they arranged social get-togethers for work teams at Medupi. Amazingly, catastrophically, it became too much trouble to do so because of the strict rules around corporate gifting and the like. The project was a feeding frenzy at the top, but you couldn't buy a six-pack of beers for hardworking construction guys without inviting a corruption probe.

Overbudget and overpriced as they are, I am still glad that Medupi and its twin in Mpumalanga Province, Kusile, will continue to power this country for decades to come. I am not happy, though, about the lies everyone had to tell to get these projects done, and the rank disrespect shown to the men who had made Eskom into one of the world's most respected power utilities. I am specifically talking about the white men.

There was an embarrassing episode with Icawa. She asked a communications agency to develop a historical narrative for the

---

233. In 2020 McKinsey also agreed to pay back 650 million rands to the state for contracts at South African Airways and Transnet, the national logistics company.

organization that showed black and white combining to build the country's electricity system. The problem was that all the historical images showed white managers and artisans standing proudly in front of their industrial works, with black laborers on the edges of the frame in a pose of subservience.

Icawa did not deal kindly with the nasty truth of our history. She blamed one of the agency men for not looking hard enough for evidence of Africans playing a proud part in Eskom's growth. To my lasting shame, I did not protest the unfair attack on him (a white Jewish man). Icawa played me very well. I disrespected myself and this honest professional in agreeing with Icawa that he was to blame for this racist depiction of Eskom's past.

Under Zuma, respect was turned on its head at Eskom as the *State Capturers* infiltrated the organization and set up their networks. How? Anton Harber explains:

> The Guptas would get the president to appoint their cronies to boards such as that of the national electricity provider, Eskom. Eskom would suddenly cancel a longstanding contract with a major coal mine, saying their coal was substandard. When the mine went into liquidation, the Guptas would buy it cheaply and sign a new, massively overpriced contract with Eskom which, in the hands of their allies, suddenly had less concern about the quality of the coal.[234]

As part of her duties to communicate useful and empowering messages to Eskom employees, Icawa did something interesting. She invited a Ghanaian woman to speak to employees about the *Daughters of Zelophehad*, an Old Testament story about how five sisters—Mahlah, Noa, Hoglah, Milcah, and Tirzah—who transform Jewish law.

---

234. (Harber, 2020, p. 116)

On Zelophehad's passing, the daughters will be denied their inheritance because the custom is that only sons inherit from the father. They petition Moses, who consults God, who decrees: "The daughters of Zelophehad are right. You shall give them possession of an inheritance among their father's brothers and transfer the inheritance of their father to them" (Numbers 25:10). The Ghanaian woman, accompanied by her proud husband, used this teaching to lecture her audience on those things the Gates couple would prefer not to talk about: monogamy, temperance, duty, honour, respect, authority, and devotion.

Icawa was in the Fengu tradition: a moderate African who wanted to work with other races to build a viable country. Yet, if merit had been the main criterion, she would not have risen this far. She had benefitted from a global agenda to boost blacks, and now she found herself relying on people like me to make her look good. Brian Dames wanted her to do the work herself, but she couldn't, so she got me to do it, paying me through a dodgy intermediary owned by a dodgy character called Gresham, whose father, David Gresham, was famous for promoting dodgy popular music.

It turns out that maybe Icawa was in the wrong job. Her father had defied apartheid restrictions to be a successful farmer, doing business with white buyers. The last time I saw Icawa she had, in the spirit of Zelophehad's daughters, followed her father's inheritance and gone into farming. She was trying to leverage the government's campaign to create black female capitalists. I did a bit of PR writing to help her raise investment funds. She assured me that even though she was African, female, and politically well-connected, this had been of scant help in navigating the bureaucratic maze to access state loans. "If this is how difficult it is for me, then I suspect the government is simply not organized enough to support any black entrepreneurship."[235]

---

235. Words to that effect.

When exactly did I finally give up hope that our African political elite could run this country for the benefit of all? It was when one of the ANC's more credible technocratic appointments, that of Brian Molefe, ended in disgrace.

Brian Molefe was active in the Struggle. When South Africa became free in 1994, he went into commerce, joining FNB (a large South African bank) before a six-year stint at the state-owned Development Bank of Southern Africa. This was followed by the plum position of CEO of the Public Investment Corporation (PIC), South Africa's state pension fund, which today manages almost R2 trillion in assets.

According to Wikipedia, under Molefe's watch as CEO of the PIC from 2003 to 2010 he "oversaw a growth in assets under management from three hundred to nine hundred billion rands. He introduced shareholder activism ... and advocated for the transformation of the South African Corporate sector to be more inclusive and representative of indigenous South Africans who had suffered under the policy of apartheid."[236] Wikipedia has noted that some of these facts *need citations*; but never mind the finer details, the statement is broadly true. Brian Molefe did indeed grow the assets under management for the PIC and was generally respected by the private sector. He is passionate about African entrepreneurship and self-reliance, and he pressured white companies to support African-run businesses as a criterion for receiving PIC funds.

Molefe moved from the PIC to head up Transnet (2011-2016), our state-owned entity in charge of rail, ports, and pipelines. He wasn't an engineer; he hadn't worked his way up through the ranks of Transnet. He had been parachuted in by a government keen to show that Africans were in charge. Not only that. Molefe espoused the Africanist ideology; he still cared about the Struggle; he cared about African dignity

---

236. (Wikipedia, 2022)

and wanted to see his people rise by their own efforts.

The first time I met him, he came to hear a talk I was giving on Herman Charles Bosman, at the National Arts Festival, which is held each year at the ultimate frontier town … Grahamstown, the center-point of the Nine Frontier Wars.

By the late 1980s, the Grahamstown Festival had become a celebration of the multiracial ideal. After 1994, when this became a reality and many cultured types left the country, the Grahamstown Festival became degraded—a symptom of South Africa's hopelessly divided sociopolitical order.

In 2018, the ANC and its Africanist allies changed the name of Grahamstown to *Makhanda*, in honour of Makhanda ka Nxele, a prototype Struggle hero who died escaping from Robben Island in the 1860s. Makhanda made his name as a warrior-prophet and was active in the Frontier Wars on the side of the *amaXhosa*.

I went to Grahamstown for decades, producing and acting in plays and enjoying the concentrated offering of arts and culture. My productions were mostly themed around the South African writer Herman Charles Bosman (1905–1951) and his contribution to literature and arts.

At the end of one of my presentations on Bosman at that 2014 festival, Molefe jumped to his feet and declaimed, "Herman Charles Bosman was a fighter for African liberation. He was on the side of the Struggle—of an African identity free of colonial baggage."[237] I didn't totally agree with him, but we had a friendly exchange on the subject. It soon struck me that this was Brian Molefe of Transnet, someone I had looked up to as a worthy helmsman steering the ship of our developmental state.

We talked afterwards. I asked if I could do some communications

---

237. Words to that effect.

work for him. A few months later I landed up in his office at the top of Carlton Centre, a fifty-story block that was once the tallest building in the Southern Hemisphere and now houses Transnet's offices.

Molefe briefed me about the themes he wanted covered for a speech he was giving in Cape Town. He was interested in the story of Onkgopotse Tiro, a black consciousness activist who was murdered by an apartheid covert unit called Z-Squad, which was part of South Africa's notorious Bureau of State Security (BOSS).[238] On 1 February 1974, the Z-Squad sent Tiro a parcel bomb, which he assumed to be from an international funding organization that would help him pay for his distance learning degree.

As president, Mandela visited Tiro's grave in Botswana in 1995, yet there was criticism that the Truth and Reconciliation Commission (TRC) had not dealt with his case, and his killers never accounted for themselves.

Molefe wanted his audience to appreciate the context of their new-found freedoms and opportunities. *Look, Tiro died so that I could take on one of the most important jobs in the country and you could get to drive in those luxury cars and eat this luxury meal.*

Molefe really did embody the hope of an Africanist elite to deliver racial redress without compromising the necessity for technocratic state-building. In 2015, he singularly embodied this hope; it seemed there were no other leading Africans who could straddle the demands of technocratic leadership with political relevance to the Africanist project.

By 2015, our state-owned enterprises—particularly our power utility Eskom—were continuing their slide downhill. There were precious few competent Africans to turn them around and there was

---

238. (South African History Online, 2019) The article cites apartheid government spy Gordon Winter's book *Inside Boss*.

precious little sense of responsibility from the Zuma-led ANC to shelve their ideology and bring in the Janissaries. So, in 2015, they made Brian Molefe CEO of Eskom, while he retained his position as CEO of Transnet. Molefe had been parachuted in as CEO of Transnet because he symbolized the Africa rising story; now he was parachuted into Eskom, while continuing to head up Transnet. In terms of the African self-reliance metric, this was worse than robbing Peter to pay Paul—it was Kafkaesque.

I once talked about Brian Molefe to the regional head of General Electric, an American. He expressed confidence in Molefe: *Here is a civil servant from the ruling party we can do business with.*

What happened during Molefe's two years as CEO of Eskom (2015–2016) ended my hope for a developmental state—my hope in the ability of an Africanist majority party to put this country on the path of state-building and political order.

In 2016, Brian Molefe resigned from Eskom after Public Protector Thuli Madonsela exposed his close ties to the Guptas in her "State of Capture" report. At the time, social media was abuzz with reports of him hanging out at the Gupta compound in Saxonwold, Johannesburg.

When the scandal emerged, I wrote him a WhatsApp message, reaching out in support I suppose. I unfortunately never got to know him very well, but I liked him. He was warm, personable, and intellectually engaged. But now with the pressure of the scandal, his intellect had become disengaged; instead of taking responsibility, he played the race card. In response to my message, he forwarded me an article by a friendly journalist arguing that he was innocent and had been the victim of those who don't want blacks to succeed.

Before that downfall, Brian Molefe invited me at the last minute to join him for a drive to Groot Marico, a small town in the North-West province—Plaatje's dry, dusty Biblical landscape. Molefe was going to visit some mutual friends (Santa and Egbert van Bart) who organize the annual Herman Charles Bosman celebrations. Alas, I had other commitments and could not go. I have not seen him since. Over the next few years events would change me. I watched something in the country dying; *a part of me dying.*

Few South African writers embraced the theme of death quite like Herman Charles Bosman (1905–1951). Bosman was an Afrikaner who became English and then wrote about Afrikaners. He also wrote sympathetically about the plight of the black man and his co-dependent relationship with the colonizer. His darkly romantic short stories are mostly set in what is today the North-West Province.[239] His first teaching position was in the remote Marico district, where Groot Marico (named for the river) is found.

It was January 1926 and Bosman would soon be twenty-one. He took with him a hunting rifle, a symbol of his manly freedom. One day, while breakfasting with his farmer hosts, he accidentally let off a shot; luckily no one was hurt. In June of 1926, he returned to Johannesburg for the holidays to stay with his mother and stepfather in a suburb called Bellevue, looking east toward the now disused Johannesburg mine dumps. His stepbrother David Russell—with whom he was not on good terms—and his younger brother, Pierre, were sharing quarters. After an argument broke out between David Russell and Pierre, Bosman intervened with his hunting rifle, killing Russell.

Bosman was so traumatized after the event, he attempted suicide—evidence of which probably helped him when, on appeal, they commuted his death sentence to ten years imprisonment, of which he served four. Bosman's mother was a Malan; her brother was Charles Malan, who was influential in South Africa's judiciary and may have

---

239. You can find Bosman's original manuscripts at the Harry Ransom Center at the University of Texas at Austin.

helped Bosman with the reprieve, after he had spent nine days on death row.

Bosman's haunting prison memoir *Cold Stone Jug* (1949) tells a dark tale of despair and redemption. But he became famous for his one hundred and fifty Marico short stories. These tales nod to the American tradition of the wry, sly, laconic backwoodsman, Bosman's iconic narrator Oom Schalk Lourens. Oom Schalk (Uncle Schalk) fought the British in both Anglo Boer wars (1880–81, 1899–1902), and fought against Plaatje's people, the Tswana, in various frontier skirmishes. He is South Africa's archetypal white man who tamed the interior for farming and cheap black labour, who gave Afrikaners a sense of their sacred purpose, an everyman version of Afrikaner founding father, Oom Paul Kruger.

Bosman and Alan Paton were contemporaries. It bugged Bosman that Paton, a reformatory headmaster, had become a literary household name with *Cry, the Beloved Country*, while he languished in obscurity after decades of artistic toil.

Bosman has something important to tell us—something that escaped Paton. This is that Africans have their own civilization, with its own potency and potential. Here, Bosman, with only the slightest hint of irony, celebrates African indigenous art.

Because they were Bushmen they had a serious understanding of the purpose of man and of his high destiny, and when they passed by, what they left behind them, on krantzes and in caves, was beauty. When we grow discouraged by the tawdry manifestations we discover in regard to the low state of development of the human mind today, it is well to reflect on the exalted achievements of a people who saw life truly and who knew better than to regard a stone merely in the light of a potential source of mineral wealth.[240]

Bosman is different from Paton in that he sees *Gotham* not as degrading to Africans but as an opportunity. "Nobody can know the streets, the gutters, the seamy side of life in a South African city like an African does." In working with this "tremendous raw material," he encouraged black writers to handle the theme romantically: "to transform this kind of squalor into the hard, imperishable grey beauty of literature."[241]

This sort of talk appealed to Brian Molefe. He was a captain of industry who patronized the arts, even if it meant hanging out in seedy places to support live music. He inspired my creative energies to write him speeches that described how his organization was fulfilling the state's vision.

In discussing Tiro's radicalization with Brian Molefe at the top of Carlton Towers, looking out across the world's richest seam of gold, the conversation took an interesting turn. A close relative of his had received poor treatment in hospital, which had sparked a conversation between Brian and his son. This son had suggested sending the hospital, "a strongly-worded letter" by way of protest. Brian Molefe was impressed at how mature and moderate the youngster was being; "The way I grew up, we would have wanted to burn something down."[242] The subject turned more generally to radicalism in the post-apartheid era. Molefe approvingly quoted the repentant poetry of Pik Botha, apartheid's longstanding foreign minister. Molefe was keen for his people to stop reliving the Struggle and instead *move on from battles we've already won.*

---

240. (Bosman, 2003, p. 101)
241. (Bosman, 2003)
242. Words to that effect.

A couple of years after that, in February 2016, Molefe's son was in the news as one of eight students at the University of Cape Town who vandalized white art in the name of the *#RhodesMustFall* movement. What had got into the mind of someone as privileged as Brian Molefe's son that he should destroy art in the name of the dubious woke cause of decolonization?

Brian Molefe is badly tainted by his connection to State Capture. Some of my friends and family gloated at his downfall: *Did you see that news story about your friend Brian Molefe hanging out at the Gupta shebeen in Saxonwold?*

There was little for me to celebrate. Molefe's reputational demise ended my hope that a *Fengu class* could steer the ship of state in advancing a winning South African civilization.

I don't want to slouch to Wakanda with Brian Molefe. It's not my cause and not my problem. My cause, my problem, is Western Civilization, and how queer it has become. The 1973 film version of *Jesus Christ Superstar* has Carl Anderson in the role of Judas, performed with soul swagger and voice to match. Anderson is black. Would our cosmopolitan producers of modern ideology cast a black Judas opposite a white Christ today? For the record, the 2000 film version of *Jesus Christ Superstar* does not have a black Judas, it has a white gay Judas, a *very* white Jesus and a mulatto Mary. This is the queer culture we in South Africa have inherited. Although I celebrate the rainbow diversity of it, I feel our national ideology lacks meatiness.

I once hoped that a Texan by the name of Don Edward Beck (1937–2022) would resolve our political crisis. In May 1995, the Texas state legislature commended Don Beck, "for his invaluable contributions toward the peaceful creation of a democratic South Africa." As his Wikipedia page tells us, Beck travelled to South Africa 36 times between 1981 and 1988 to meet leaders from business, labour, and politics, sharing his vision for a harmonious and prosperous South Africa.

Beck's theory of Spiral Dynamics is explained in his 1996 book, co-written with Christopher Cowan, *Spiral Dynamics: Mastering Values, Leadership and Change.*[243] Ken Wilber leans on Spiral Dynamics for his book *A Theory of Everything: An Integral Vision for Business, Politics, Science, and Spirituality* (2000). Wilber and Beck are mapmakers of the human soul, optimists who believe that humanity is on a spiritual journey. The academy does not take Wilber's ideas seriously, but he is influential in other circles, garnering a worldwide fanbase of millions, including Bill Clinton.

I first came across Wilber in the early 1990s. I found him to be a breath of fresh air, a timely riposte to the tired theories they teach in sociology departments. I liked the fact that Wilber is not only an intellectual—he is also a meditator and a mystic.

South Africa in the 1980s was the ideal place to road-test some of Beck's and Wilber's ideas. Don Beck believed that South Africa should do away with its racial hierarchy, but not do away with the idea of hierarchy altogether. "It's not the color *of* the person, it's the color *in* the person," he would tell listeners. Those internal colors (beige, purple, red, blue, orange, green, yellow, turquoise) are Spiral Dynamics code for different stages of psychosocial becoming.

It's hard not to fall into parody when describing Beck's vision for sociopolitical order, with its strange color hierarchy.[244] But people like Beck and Wilber are making a crucial point: adults—not only children—also go through stages of moral development.

Unfortunately, applying Spiral Dynamics to South Africa

---

243. Cowan and Beck eventually fell out about Spiral Dynamics; today they represent two distinct strands of the philosophy.

244. Beck had his eccentricities, naming his laptop *Sparky*, because conferring a personality on it would, he hoped, make it work better.

reinforces taboo notions of racial hierarchy. The model tends to typify indigenous peoples as belonging to the lower tribal bands of the spiral (beige, purple and red), while Europeans and Asians cluster at the mid-range mythic stage (blue) or the scientific (orange) and humanist (green) stages above it. It piqued me that the father of our old nation, Jan Smuts, had developed his own paradigm of spiritual evolution mirroring this one: Holism. Smuts anticipated the transpersonal humanist movement, of which Wilber is a key figure.[245]

For a concerned liberal who was disillusioned with the narrow ideology of humanities discourse, Wilber and Beck presented a heady alternative. If children go through stages of intellectual and moral development, as Piaget showed, then why can't adults do likewise? Why can't they transcend the limits of their earlier belief systems to become more open, flexible thinkers who can better respond to the complexities of our time?

Beck's inspiration for how this happens came from Clare Graves, a professor in psychology at Union College, New York, who in 1981 published a paper titled The Emergent, Cyclical, Double-Helix Model of the Adult Human Biopsychosocial Systems.

Whatever the faults of these transpersonal models, they do at least articulate a modern version of perennial religious ideas. Graves adds a quasi-spiritual dimension to his framework. The lower levels are part of the *subsistence* tier; the higher levels are in the *being* tier. He describes the attitude of someone in the being tier: "My way does not have to be yours, nor yours mine, yet I have very strong convictions about what is my way, but never such about yours."[246] This sounds like the attitude you need in South Africa to prevent yourself from going nuts.

Which is why I reached out to Don Beck at a time when the country

---

245. Wilber does acknowledge Smuts, if only in passing, in his writings.
246. (Graves, 1981)

was in crisis. It was 2014, we were in the midst of State Capture. My day job was to ghostwrite for captains of industry. I could sense their frustration and hopelessness at blatant looting of state resources from the top. The situation proved that the standard ways for understanding society and politics could not explain what was going on. Who else could speak to such extraordinary circumstances but Don Beck, the man who—along with Ken Wilber—had an actual explanation as to why President Jacob Zuma was behaving like a lascivious tribal potentate and not a head of state?

I wanted Don Beck to return to South Africa and share his understandings. But then I came across an article in which he lamented that his recommendations during the transition back in the 1980s had been ignored. According to Beck, South Africa was better off under apartheid. I wrote him saying he should withdraw such a statement; not only was it untrue, but it would also disqualify him as a voice of reason in our ongoing attempts to heal this land. Not even the outspoken opposition leader Helen Zille would say such a thing. In fact she often makes a point of stating the opposite. The late Archbishop Desmond Tutu, perhaps, had the moral authority to make such a sweeping claim, but not Don Beck.

Beck did not back down from his statement and continued to express interest in returning to South Africa. It could have been a much-deserved swansong. However, after this incident, and after having made a few calls to friends in high places, I was disabused of the idea. It seemed like Beck was no longer that welcome here.

Beck had warned that majority rule could degrade the country. In fact, his model predicted it. His greatest concern was that not enough black Africans were entering the blue stage of development, which in the East and the West had been ushered by the age of literacy and great religions: Hinduism, Judaism, Christianity, Buddhism, and Islam.

Beck lamented, *where is the blue in Africa? I am not seeing the blue, when is it going to come through?*[247] Beck was concerned that well-meaning liberal westerners were applying a once-size-fits-all ideology to Africa, with little acknowledgement of the fact that Africa is much more tribal than Europe.

It might seem controversial to claim that much of South Africa is locked in the narrow worldview of tribalism, yet South African customary law—based on tribal custom—is protected by our constitution in recognition of the pluralistic nature of our society.[248] Tribalism is a legal fact in this country.

The uncomfortable truth was that Beck did not rate very highly the leading lights of the African liberation movement. He did not see them as being any higher on the spiral than our white apartheid leaders, whom he typified as being in that God-fearing blue stage. Beck's appraisal has proved to be true. Our African political elite have disappointed the country. There main achievement is African solidarity, a sort of pan-tribalism to defend against white power.

I attended the official Spiral Dynamics course (Beck's version) in South Africa, run by Mandala Consulting. The course was conducted by Loraine Laubscher, a pioneer of the paradigm who had met Graves. Mandala contracted themselves out to the mines, applying the paradigm to help mine bosses understand the perplexities of African tribalism. I had a conversation with one of these bosses who was steeped in the paradigm. He told me that many African workers looked to the company as their *father*. I assume he meant that to these workers, the company represented an authoritarian God who could make or break

---

247. A friend of mine attests to an anecdote Beck told, whereby he consulted to President FW de Klerk, who joked with him: *Am I orange enough for you?* Or it may have been: *Am I blue enough for you?*

248. In the late 70s the apartheid government use the term *plural relations* to describe apartheid. Some joked that blacks were now *plurals*.

them, yet who was generally consistent and just.[249]

I asked Loraine what she thought of Zuma (this was when he was president). He was *low purple*, i.e. so deeply tribal as to be incapable of having a vision for the country he was meant to be leading. That proved to be true enough.

She was acquainted with our current president, Cyril Ramaphosa, whom she got to know when he was building the country's most powerful trade union in the 1980s, the National Union of Mineworkers. Dr. Loraine Laubscher was rather iffy about Ramaphosa and did not rate him as being particularly high on the spiral either, although I can't remember exactly where she put him. Laubscher, who died in 2020, was the sort of white South African who was both intellectually interested in how the country was unfolding, as well as engaged with the actual events of its unfolding. Her paradigm was outside the academy and outside received wisdom of the liberal elites who govern world institutions. She was a free thinker who was fluent in Sotho, which is spoken widely on South Africa's gold belt. It seems she had been employed by these mines because she could get inside the heads of those with a tribal worldview.

At the end of the course, by way of tribute to Loraine Laubscher, the director of Mandala told us an anecdote about her. A mine had been having problems with employees aiding and abetting illegal mining. They suspected a certain middle manager might be involved, but they couldn't prove anything. Laubscher sniffed the guy out and then confronted him, in Sotho, telling him that unless he desisted, she would use her witch powers to curse him: the death of his cattle and the destruction of his homestead would ensue. The man broke down and confessed.

If we're going to deal with tribal leaders, then we need to learn the

---

249. This did not prevent them from striking rather regularly.

tricks of tribal communication. Loraine Laubscher epitomizes Graves's description of the most open—yet grounded—personality, someone who, "Accepts and lives with the fact of differences."[250] When I met her, she was well into her 80s, yet she retained a strong intellectual curiosity and had an original outlook. She had little faith in South Africa working out per its current setup, speculating that we would have been better off had there been a communist takeover. She was no fan of communism, but she perhaps believed that the country needed something as drastic as the secular religion of communism to shift the masses into the blue stage.

The Beck-Wilber vision for South Africa is now being taken forward by the Integral Africa Institute, a collection of business consultants that includes Mandala's director, Rica Viljoen. If their poorly written website is anything to go by, they have little to offer in the way of sociopolitical solutions. "In a world that is currently being driven by increasingly radical splits it is more and more imperative to connect ourselves to the earth, each other, all sentient beings, and to the universe, in a cosmic embrace to make up the greater whole."[251]

What would Jan Smuts say about his finely tuned theory being repurposed as New Age woo-woo?

---

250. (Graves, 1981)
251. (Integral African Conference, 2020)

IN THE NAME OF SMUTS

There was a time when we respected the genius in men. Jan Smuts is the towering figure of white South Africa, the man who invented the country and then lived long enough to watch his Boers *crucify* him, as he lamented in 1948 when the Afrikaners voted his party out of power.

In 1901 Smuts sentenced a man to death, Lemuel Colyn, by firing squad. It was during the Anglo-Boer War, at Clanwilliam, in the far west of the country. Colyn infiltrated Smuts's Boer guerilla ranks and then betrayed their position to the British occupiers. When Colyn fell to Smuts's feet pleading for mercy, the general told him, "For you Colyn, there can be no mercy!" Smuts presided over the court-martialing of Colyn, sentencing him to death.

Smuts wrote the blueprint for the country and then ruled over it in the first half of the twentieth century. For an American equivalent, we must look to a Jefferson rolled up with Lincoln. After the Union of South Africa in 1910, Smuts was right hand man to Prime Minister Louis Botha. In the first few years of Union he simultaneously headed up three ministries: interior, mines, and defence. As defence minister he personally led troops in the First World War against the Germans in East Africa. When Botha died in 1919, Smuts took over as prime minister, before losing the 1924 election to JBM Hertzog's National Party. Smuts was back in government in 1934, when his South African Party merged with the National Party to form the United Party. In 1939–1948 Smuts was again prime minister, the country's last pre-apartheid leader.

Smuts was a gradualist about race; he called apartheid a *klomp nonsens* (load of nonsense) and as early as 1942, he declared *segregation has fallen on evil days*.

But he stood firm in his support for political segregation, or what some might call *white supremacy*. As a response to African political aspiration, he promoted instead "practical social policy away from politics" (1945).[252] Smuts did not believe in politics for the African masses—not really for the African elite either. Instead, he wanted to placate them with favourable social policy and limited political rights.

Smuts was a central figure in the government's policy of taking land from Africans and giving it to Europeans. He was under no illusions about the colonial conquest of a territory, acknowledging in 1906, "the Native races whose land it was long before we came here to force a policy of dispossession on them." He was a leading figure behind the Natives Land Act (1913), which gave the white government wide-ranging powers to evict Africans from the land of their ancestors, turning independent African farmers into laborers and servants for whites. John Dube fumed in *Ilanga Lase Natal* (his newspaper) that the law was a message to Africans telling them to: "Get out, *Fotesake* (go-away), Go back to your locations, or else go back to work for your white masters."[253] This travesty was Smuts' doing.

Who was this man who dispossessed his own citizens while being

---

252. In a letter to his deputy, Jan Hofmeyr (1945)
253. https://www.sahistory.org.za/article/natives-land-act-1913

lionized internationally as a humanitarian and global statesman? Whom Churchill during World War II referred to as "that wonderful man, with his immense profound mind, and his eye watching from a distance the whole panorama of European affairs?" Afrikaner nationalists hated Smuts for his vanity, his Anglophilia, his grand vision of world government; they should have thanked him for not being as suicidally racist as the apartheid leaders who came after him. He believed Afrikaner and English should unite in creating a *bulwark for European civilization* in Africa.

South Africa is a Frankenstein's monster of a nation. It staggers on, mainly because of the momentum of eighty-four years of state-building that was inspired by principles we no longer care about. Immediately after drawing up the world's most liberal and democratic constitution in 1994, the state proceeded to systematically degrade it, making a mockery of the principles on which the new South Africa was founded.

Jan Smuts was right, we are here to build a bulwark for civilization. We've allowed the state to become infiltrated by barbaric attitudes. We've allowed it to become degraded and polluted.

The fashion with the professional-managerial class is to reduce all problems to technocratic issues, as the Bill and Melinda Gates Foundation does. The technocrats assure us that robust economic growth and sound developmental policy is all South Africa needs. This has it back to front. Economy is not the purpose of a nation, and not the true cause of national development. Rather, economic growth is the happy accident of Fukuyama's triumvirate: state-building, rule of law, and accountable government.

What's the barometer of South Africa's failure? The proportion of the professional-managerial class, that priesthood of dynamic modern economies, who are looking for opportunities elsewhere. We're losing more people from this class than we're gaining. Only when that equation is reversed will there be room for hope. Smuts' bulwark is crumbling. Could it have been any other way?

In 1946, ANC president Alfred B. Xuma bumped into Jan Smuts at a press conference in New York City. Xuma had been trying to meet Smuts, but the South African prime minister was not interested in discussing political rights for Africans. As legend has it, Xuma took the chance to joke with Smuts: "I have had to fly ten thousand miles to meet my prime minister. He talks about us but won't talk to us."

In a parallel world, I'd like to imagine that Smuts sat down and listened while Xuma unburdened his heart and that Smuts—on losing the 1948 election—grasped his terrible mistake and owned up to it. That when he died, this letter was read out at the United Nations:

> I, Jan Christiaan Smuts, have but a few months left on this earth. And when I die, so too will die a link to much of our history. I am the last living member of Kruger's government, the last senior general of the Anglo-Boer War, the last Minister of the Old Transvaal Colonial Government, the last of the signatories to the Treaty of Versailles, and the last member of the War Cabinet of the First World War.

> It was I who persuaded British prime minister Henry Campbell-Bannerman in 1905 to return the Boer Republics of the Transvaal and the Orange Free State to self-rule. It was I who wrote the founding constitution of South Africa and then had it ratified by the British in 1909. The British government pressed the issue of franchise for the Africans, but I persuaded them that there was no need to extend the vote to black people in the Transvaal, the Free State and Natal, and that white South Africans would treat Africans with honour and dignity—as proper citizens of the country.

I gave my word to the British, and they in turn gave us the country—only eight years after the bitter Boer defeat at the hands of the Empire. We lost the war but thanks in no small measure to my good relations with the British, we won the peace. We Afrikaners sought only self-rule in the Orange Free State and in the Transvaal and yet we received so much more. From 1910, we practically had the run of the entire country, including Natal and the Cape Province. At the time, I exclaimed, "They gave us back, in everything but name, our country. After four years! Has such a miracle of trust and magnanimity ever happened before?"

As deputy to Prime Minister Louis Botha in 1914 and then as prime minister in 1939, I twice took South Africa into war on the side of our British allies, on the side of Western values. Twice, we defeated the forces of extreme nationalism.

Besides being instrumental in establishing the Union of South Africa in 1910, I was also singularly responsible for establishing the League of Nations. I am the only person to have signed the charters of both the League of Nations and the United Nations, and I wrote the Preamble of the United Nations Charter, which was unfortunately edited not entirely to my liking. I point you to those opening words: "We, the peoples of the United Nations, determined to save succeeding generations from the scourge of war, which twice in our lifetime has brought untold sorrow to mankind, and to reaffirm faith in fundamental human rights, in the dignity and worth of the human person..." This is a mistake; my original phrasing was *human personality* not *human person*. I believe in the sacred evolving dynamism of the human personality.

As I wrote in 1927, "In the last resort a civilisation depends on its general ideas; it is nothing but a spiritual structure of the dominant ideas expressing themselves in institutions and the subtle atmosphere of culture. If the soul of our civilisation is to be saved we shall have to find new and fuller expression for the great saving unities."[254] Unity is built on justice.

I created this country in the image of a just divinity, or rather I sought to do so. My vision was for a humane country that would deal justly with the weak and dispossessed.

When the National Party took power from me in 1948, I had occasion to rethink my political shortcomings. I believe that apartheid will forever stain the soul of the Afrikaner. Where once Afrikaners were admired as a freedom-loving people who stood up to the worst of imperialism, in future they will be known primarily for the evil done in the name of apartheid. I will be remembered as the man who unwittingly gave the country to those who are against the evolving spiritual advancement of the human *personality*. All the good I have done will be overshadowed by the very infamy of this policy of strict segregation.

The central evil of South Africa today is that Africans must rely on the goodness of whites for their grievances to be heard. Their lack of political power means that they are essentially outsiders in their own land; there is little incentive for a white government to treat them justly. The National Party appealed to the very worst in human nature—greed, exclusiveness, fear, and hate—wrapped up in a perverse theology. This policy of apartheid is a repudiation of Britain's deal with white South Africa in 1909. It is not only wrong and evil but, as I see it, illegitimate too.

Therefore, on my death I want it known to the world—particularly to Britain who bequeathed this country in trust to the white

254. (Smuts, 1927)

population—that my name must not bolster the legitimacy of this system. And that all sensible people who care about this country should do whatever it takes to put South Africa on the path to some sort of normality in relations between the races. South Africa will only join the community of civilized nations when the original sin of political exclusion of blacks is corrected and when legitimate representatives of the different races enter into a power-sharing agreement, as fellow children of one fatherland.

Unfortunately, Smuts never wrote such a letter. He never developed that viable middle road between white supremacy and African majority rule. He eroded the foundations of his own bulwark of civilization.

With his upright pose and philosophic gaze, Jan Smuts is a much-copied act in these parts. But not for his racial views—thankfully. Smuts believed the white race was destined to lead *lesser* ones: "We see in one [Europeans] the leading race of the world, while the other [Bushmen/Khoisan], though still living, has become a mere human fossil, verging on extinction. We see the one crowned with all the intellectual and spiritual glory of the race, while the other still occupies the lowest scale in human existence." Smuts had every reason to feel proud of himself and the achievements of his race.

At school, we had a coveted prize known as the Rex Pennington Award for All-Round Achievement. It went to the boy who accomplished the most across various fields during his five years at high school. If the gods of the twentieth century decide to run their own *Rex Pennington Award for All-Round Achievement*, Jan Smuts has a good chance of winning, considering his résumé:

✓ Cambridge University's smartest law student

✓ One of the world's greatest guerrilla war strategists: in the second part of the Anglo-Boer War, with only 400 men, Smuts suckers half the British army

✓ Co-founder of the Union of South Africa and twice its prime minister

✓ Key in establishing the country as an industrial African power

✓ A leading general on the winning side in both World Wars

✓ Founder of the Royal Air Force

✓ *Cassandra* at the Treaty of Versailles (1919), predicting to exactitude the consequences of punishing Germany too harshly

✓ Prophet of world government: driving force behind the League of Nations, the United Nations, and the Commonwealth

✓ Hangs out with Churchill … and Gandhi

✓ Biologist: discovers species of African grasses, one— *Smutsfinger*—is named for him

✓ Scientist: Albert Einstein says Smuts is one of only a handful of people who truly get $e=mc2$

✓ Prescient literary critic: his book, *Walt Whitman: A Study in the Evolution of the Personality*, written in 1895, anticipates the New Age spiritual movement[255]

✓ Philosopher: his book *Holism and Evolution* (1926) continues the theme of evolution and culture as spiritual phenomena made meaningful by character development and personal growth

✓ *Don Juan*: He has intense affairs of the heart with numerous interesting women, including with World War II celebrity Princess Frederica of Hanover, who is young enough to be his granddaughter.

---

255. Smuts acknowledged Whitman for helping him overcome his Calvinist sexual repression.

It's 1948; Smuts is seventy-eight years old. The century is not even halfway through, but in an unprecedented move the Rex Pennington Committee decides not to wait it out. No one can catch Smuts—not in fifty years, not in five hundred years—and so they give him the coveted *Rex Pennington Award for All Round Achievement in the Twentieth Century*. Naturally, Smuts is proud. He is excessively proud. He forgets that he is a mortal, in essence no different than the naked coloured people wandering the *Kgalagadi* (Kalahari) of whom he thinks so little. Thanks to his efforts on the world stage, the country is a beacon of success against the backdrop of a ruined Europe.

The gods note Smuts' hubris and out of kindness they send him a warning. In January 1948, Mahatma Gandhi is assassinated. The great general sheds a quiet tear. He remembers Gandhi not only as a formidable foe in the political arena but as a philosophical kindred spirit. He calls to his wife Isie, "Bring me my sandals"—the very sandals Gandhi made for him in 1911 while a prisoner of Smuts' government. Isie brings him the sandals and goes back to her ironing. He lovingly cradles the sandals, reminiscing about his great rival who is no more.

But Smuts does not heed this portent; he cannot be surpassed. On 25 May 1948, the gods decide to bring the *Oubaas* to his knees and take his beloved country down with him.[256] Excessive pride may seem but a peccadillo in the earthly realm, but to the gods it is taboo. With far fewer votes than Smuts, DF Malan *steals* Smuts' throne. Malan's Herenigde Nasionale Party puts an eight-track cassette into the deck and rewinds history.

Smuts is devastated. His political life's work in South Africa is the United Party, and now the Afrikaner nationalists sweep it from power for good. He cries out: "My Afrikaners have turned against me—they have crucified me."

---

256. *Oubaas: old boss.*

The gods are just getting started. In October of that year, Smuts' beloved son and heir, Japie, dies of cerebral meningitis. And then the United Nations begins its unrelenting attack on white-ruled South Africa.

But Smuts has hope yet . . . he has Hofmeyr, Jan Hendrik Hofmeyr—the *Little Prince of South African politics*—the man who will finish Smuts' work of binding Afrikaner and English in the cause of securing Western Civilization its bulwark on the African continent.

Hofmeyr is the minister of finance, minister of education, and deputy prime minister. He is quietly running the country during the war years while Smuts is fighting fascism ... and trying to bed Princess Frederica.[257]

Hofmeyr—an intellectual fixer who performs administrative miracles—is important to Smuts' leadership. Had South Africa been on the side of the Nazis during World War II, Hofmeyr would have been Smuts' *Albert Speer*—but that's another story.

Hofmeyr is quite unlike Smuts. He is short and stocky; he wears thick glasses and lives with his mother. Hofmeyr loves cricket, cats, and Christ. His holidays are spent camping with the boys of the Student Christian Association on the Natal South Coast, as always, accompanied by his mother.[258]

Underneath the herculean intellect is a little boy who never grows up. If you want to understand Hofmeyr you can read Alan Paton's *Hofmeyr* (1964)—all one thousand pages of it. Or you can spend a few minutes reading Herman Charles Bosman's report of an interview he conducted with Hofmeyr. Bosman is South Africa's preeminent humorist, our very own *Mark Twain*. He interviews Hofmeyr, who

---

257. He may have tried to bed other young women too, as Piet Beukes attests in his biographical accounts of the man.
258. Alan Paton would join on those excursions until he became put off by them (he did not say why).

is standing for parliament, a few months before those fateful 1948 elections.[259] As always, Bosman gets to the soul of the matter. It is not Hofmeyr's famous liberalism, not his domineering mother, nor his complex relationship with Smuts that Bosman focuses on. Instead, Bosman pronounces on Hofmeyr's cats. He writes:

> If you are interested, Hofmeyr has four cats—a white Persian, a Siamese and two very mixed breed black cats. They travel backwards and forwards between Pretoria and Cape Town with Jan H. and his mother, and their names are poetry. The oldest is Juba—who has travelled more than twenty thousand miles in his time, and enjoys travelling—and Net So (twin to Ook So, now deceased), and Ulysses the Siamese, and Nicodemus, so named because "he came by night." All this may sound trivial, but I can only say that the New Testament reference, combined with the thought of that unwanted black cat that one night found shelter, left me not unmoved.[260]

After the cat chitchat, Hofmeyr expands on his philosophy for life: "Success in life means only one thing to me. And that lies in the degree to which you have been of service to others." Bosman follows with his own thoughts: "Hofmeyr spoke these words with a sincerity that there was no denying, and that made me cough against the back of my hand."

Bosman is indeed convinced of Hofmeyr's sincerity, for this is how he ends the piece:

> I hope that Jan Hendrik Hofmeyr gets in at Johannesburg North. Because the man who is standing against him, Fritz Steyn, is a big game hunter. I hate all people who destroy animals—Nimrod and Selous and the rest of them. Shooting at creatures that can't shoot back. Give me a man that says,

259. It was for *Trek* magazine.
260. (Bosman, 2003)

"Enter and welcome" to a homeless black cat scratching on his back door in the night.[261]

When Bosman heard the news of that apartheid election victory, he spontaneously threw his hat to the ground. Had white South Africans supported Hofmeyr, we could have achieved political integration and built a country that all races could be proud of. The National Party had other ideas, coming up with apartheid and painting a target on white South Africa for everyone to shoot at. A sport which continues to this day.

---

261. (Bosman, 2003)

IN THE NAME OF THE FATHER

Charles Rawden Maclean, better known as John Ross, was a young Scot who would have agreed with Bosman's general sentiment. Maclean was shipwrecked in Port Natal in September 1825. For three of his adolescent years he lived in Shaka's kingdom; most of that time spent as guest of the court of *uShaka*.[262]

At the time of the shipwreck he was only twelve or thirteen, the youngest crewmember of the *Mary,* a brig captained by James King. Maclean wrote of his three-year adventure there in a piece titled "Loss of the Brig *Mary* in Natal" (1853).

Maclean was later memorialized as John Ross, a mythical pioneering figure who saves the white settlement by walking 600 miles to fetch supplies in Delagoa Bay (now the Mozambican capital of Maputo). We Natal kids were taught this legend, which was brought to life by a beautiful bronze of John Ross, at John Ross House, near Durban harbour.

I point you to Stephen Gray's publication of *The Natal Papers of John Ross* (1992). Here you can read Maclean's extraordinary account of being shipwrecked among savages. A child slips through the veil

262. In Nguni languages the correct way to address someone is with the prefix *u*.

of civilization and spends months as a lone white figure advising the savage king. For once, the real story is bigger than the myth.

When the handful of shipwrecked sailors make their way to Shaka's court to pay homage, Shaka offers them hospitality and support before sending them away to repair their ship. All but one ... the young Charles Maclean. On hearing the news, Maclean tells us that his heart "sank with despair at the horror of being left alone in the midst of this wild and terrible scene, cut off from all communion, all intercourse and even the sight of civilization."[263]

But then after a short while, he is taken into Shaka's confidence, telling readers, "I had extraordinary power and influence with the savage chief. Mine, indeed, was a strange destiny."[264]

Was Maclean a young Kurtz of Conrad's *Heart of Darkness*, manipulating his privileged position to dominate the natives? No, the young Maclean embodies the Christian pity of our civilization: "I can recall to mind the day when my feeble voice, raised in the distant wilderness of Africa, stayed the bloody hand of a relentless executioner from destroying many innocent victims."[265] Indeed, Maclean comments on the essential innocence of his Zulu hosts: "Were I called upon to state in which condition the most happiness existed, I should, from the knowledge I have of man in both conditions, bear testimony to the Zulus being the most cheerful and happy people of which I have had any experience."[266]

Our liberal humanist order is founded on nothing more than the good faith shown to a red-headed Scots kid by simple Zulu folks and their king. That should be justification enough for committed liberals. Out of love and an attempt to comprehend otherness—and in honour

---

263. (Maclean & Gray, 1996, p. 196) Slightly paraphrased.
264. (Maclean & Gray, 1996)
265. (Maclean & Gray, 1996, p. 113)
266. (Maclean & Gray, 1996, p. 196)

of Maclean—we reaffirm the rights of indigenous peoples as members of the human family.

But what happens when everything we care about in this civilization is up for grabs because we daren't come across as *racist*?

We will not right the wrongs by falling in with *antiracism* ideology. Events in Ukraine prove once again that humans are equally capable of oppressing those of their own race. White guilt, posturing antiracism, cultural relativism, denial of the primacy of Western Civilization— these are the sins of modernity. These are Nietzsche's *sacred games* to *comfort ourselves* at having killed God.[267]

We cannot meet the demands of the Gcaleka-Xhosa in their struggle for tribal pride. We cannot turn the clock back and reinstate the tribal authority of a Hintsa. We can only be true to our own civilization—our own values. It's not up to non-Africans to manufacture an African civilization out of nothing and to confer racial pride by fiat. It's for Africans to define and build their own civilization. We cannot affirm *blackness* or *Africaness* by means of moral book-balancing. This will not assuage the guilt of privilege. Nor will it remove the burden of responsibility that privilege confers.

Today you can visit John Ross's birthplace in Scotland and pay homage at his shrine. I hope to do so one day. But for now, allow me to channel his spirit to tell us how to save our beloved land.

I, John Ross, born Charles Rawden Maclean, spent three years in the kingdom of *uShaka*, one of Africa's great tribal leaders. What can I tell of the man? His subtlety and intelligence come immediately to mind, his ability to sit naked among a thousand of his fiercest warriors and yet exude ultimate power and ease over his domain, lecturing them for hours on end, his incanta-

---

267. From a widely quoted Nietzsche passage.

tions punctuated with the humming refrain of *yebo Baba, yebo Baba, yebo Baba* ... (yes Father)

Was he a father figure to me? There can be little doubt that he was a father of the nation and as one of his subjects I was his son. The relationship went beyond that though, as I could glimpse his vulnerabilities, which he felt freer to share with someone who posed so little threat to him. I believe that had I stayed in his court for longer or become permanently installed there as an official advisor to the potentate, I could have ameliorated the suffering visited on those felicitous people by their ruler after the death of his mother *uNandi*.

I am heartened that South Africa now has a universalist constitution in which the natural rights and freedom of men and women, of all races, are guaranteed.

But I fear that now with universal emancipation achieved your civilization is self-destructing. It seems you underestimated what a painstaking process it is to build a civilization. As I once put it, "the progress of civilization is slow, and all attempts to force it only increases the obstacles and adds to the obstinacy of those who are opposed to it."[268] You overestimated the appeal of civilization and you underestimated the natural pull of the tribal order, which I can attest is better suited to the happiness of humanity. It was not politically incorrect to say so back then—I would put it differently were I writing today—but my point from that 1853 article still stands: "I believe it easier for an ignorant man, in fact, more properly speaking, for human nature to relapse into a state of barbarism than it is to advance a savage to a state of civilization."[269]

---

268. (Maclean & Gray, 1996, p. 130)
269. Ibid, slightly paraphrased

Your civilization is more fragile than you imagine. From my exalted vantage point, I see it slipping through your fingers. Not because of your efforts to edify the indigenous and include them in your civilizing project. No, this was not the downfall of your civilization, to the contrary, it remains a potent antidote to the horrors of sectarianism.

Once was when you were proud to share in the achievements of your race; proud to trumpet the fact that European science had transformed the world into a place worthy of infinite wonder and enquiry; proud that your religion pioneered universal ethics, casting a blanket of Christian care over the downtrodden.

In 1846, in Wilmington, North Carolina, I threatened to shoot harbor authorities who would enslave my black crew members. I protested the cruel treatment of Langalibalele, imprisoned on Robben Island in the 1870s for resisting colonial inequities. We wanted a fair trial for Langalibalele, to whom I felt responsible, given that a namesake of his had opened his heart to me at a time when I could not have been more vulnerable. As I put it, "those are yet living to whom I am indirectly indebted for my life", rightly, their goodness should "meet a just reward by kindness and forbearance at the white man's hands which I experienced at their hands in the day of their rule." I was "a decided advocate for his [Langalibalele's] liberty, in common with that of the whole African race." [270]

I thought that the Zulus would one day disappear like *snow in the rain*. *uShaka* thought that the *swallows* (Europeans) would eventually overrun his kingdom. The great chief acknowledged King George as *King of the whites*, as long as he could be *King of the blacks*. What would he make of your situation, overlapping *kingdoms* sharing a nation?

---

270. (Maclean & Gray, 1996, p. 144)

When I settled on that beautiful island of St Lucia in the Caribbean I became a stipendiary magistrate, mediating between the community of recently freed slaves and white settlers. The job came naturally to me; I was a true foot-soldier of integration.

I rose to become a respected Ship's Captain—in the time of slavery and sugar. I chose to oppose slavery but not sugar, which I dutifully shipped from those West Indian islands to the glorious centre of Empire. In God, Empire, and sugar, alas, I trusted.

No . . . let me rephrase. I am proud of what I did for King, country, and family. If my cause over-stimulated the palate of a bored Imperial elite, fueling their heretical musings, then let God judge me. But I stood for the best of Empire, its compassionate heart, its subtle renderings of the Holy Word in whose name I invoked "the genius of universal emancipation—that which has set her foot in every land, below which slavery must be forever trodden down." I am gratified that today, everyone's rights as members of the human family have been vindicated and, as I prophesied, "the pseudo-Christianity that reduces Native Africans to the condition of the brute creation has lost ground." [271]

In 1853 and again in 1875 I testified to the Empire my position on what became known as *the native problem*, or *the native question*, what you now simply call *race*. My grounds for begging fair treatment and equal rights on behalf of the indigenous was not a repudiation of my decision to live and work with them. To the contrary, I am proud to have been an emissary of enlightened British values. In short, civilization has no equal; it is the preferred constellation by which we guide the

271. (Maclean & Gray, 1996)

ship across a dark ocean. As I put it: "If we are to deplore the darkness in which he is placed as regards his future and eternal happiness and misery, we must at the same time bear in mind *that of him to whom much is given much will be required*, and how much we may have to answer for who have so large a share of the talents that the Lord gave to his servants, and how better it may be for the savage in that day of account than for many of us."[272]

I know you cringe at the word *savage* and the patronizing tone of my message. In my defense, it was 1875, what else could I say, and how else could I say it? There were real atrocities going on, like what we see in Ukraine today. Hordes slaughtering innocent people—as I highlighted in that *Times* article: "The cruel and bloody aggressions of the Boers on the Natives have engendered feelings of hatred and retaliation in the breasts of the simple and untutored natives." I predicted that "this would raise feelings in the minds of the Natives that would be long remembered and lead to barbarities reciprocal and terrific."[273]

You had an ancestral debt to pay—instead you allowed the Boer spirit of racial conquest to prevail. As I warned, "Many years of kind treatment will be required to blot out the atrocities perpetrated by people professing the doctrines of Christianity."[274]

How do you repay the debt? Not by kowtowing to the tribal instincts that infect your institutions. Whether you know it or not, there is a Godly crown at the center of your civilization. The only debt worth repaying is obeisance to it.

---

272. (Maclean & Gray, 1996) Italics is Luke 12:48 (Maclean's original does not cite the Biblical reference for the quotation).
273. (Maclean & Gray, 1996) Slightly paraphrased.
274. (Maclean & Gray, 1996, p. 74)

The genius of universal emancipation is a rare gift that your world has inverted, turning the sacred cross into a carnival of heresy.

As a callow Scots lad I raised my voice against blood sacrifice perpetrated by *uShaka*—on whose authority was I doing so? It was on the authority of the Christian God, the same God the Boers honored when they defeated Dingaan ... not quite the same.

My authority is the Christian God of pity and progress, mercy and science. But never mind your duty to God—I leave that to your conscience—you have a duty to me, to all those who came before, to redeem our sacrifices, to emulate our encouraging, adventurous, masculine spirit.[275]

Your country belongs to that class of Man which shares a divine instinct for civilization, a devotion to truth and goodness, a posture of reason and intellectual curiosity.

In the name of the Father, there is not only shame in your civilization, there is edification and glory in it too.

---

275. I borrow this phrase "encouraging, adventurous, masculine spirit" from Jordan Peterson.

POSTSCRIPT

13 October 2022, Ferndale, Johannesburg.

I am now free of much of the cognitive dissonance that got me writing this book in the first place. An African majority government will always be encouraged to build a pan-tribal alliance whose essential feature is race. We have to defend the country against this debasement of our constitutional values. If African ruling elites refuse to play by the rules of our constitution, then we must take responsibility for enforcing the rights and freedoms enshrined in that document.

That's why I joined AfriForum, a citizens' rights organization, focusing mainly on the interests of Afrikaners. Yesterday I went to my first meeting, where neighborhood security, municipal indifference, and environmental cleanups were the topics. I heard from people who were doing something about these problems within their community. I felt safe. More than that, I felt myself to be less bitter and angry about our predicament than I have in years.

After this convivial and interesting encounter with people mostly of my race, I took myself off to a nearby nature reserve. Here the racial demographics were the opposite, but this felt to be of little consequence. People were enjoying a slice of South Africa's beautiful bushveld, some having driven only minutes from their homes, made possible—in part—by the sacrifices of those at the AfriForum meeting. *Parents and children enjoying community and nature in a safe and pristine setting.* This is civilization.

There is nothing to be angry about. When you have reason and justice on your side—not to mention your enshrined constitutional right to citizenship—then who can stand in your way?

Get off your screens and go out and make connections with nature and with the people around you. Evil has many faces in these weird times. But it mostly comes in the form of a vacant screen stealing our attention and selling it back to us as broken bits of our forgotten personalities. If you're looking for a reason to get involved—to *get your voice back*—I leave you with the opening paragraph of AfriForum's civil rights charter:

> We—the compilers and supporters of this charter—exercise the deliberate choice to meaningfully and permanently exist freely, safely and prosperously as Afrikaners, with our deeply-rooted foundation at the southern tip of Africa. We know no other home. This right to a meaningful existence extends to all communities and we are pleased to cooperate in seeking a better future for all. In exercising this choice of continued existence, we are inspired by the same universal values of freedom, equality and justice for all. [276]

---

276. (AfriForum, 2019) *Get your voice back* is an AfriForum slogan.

BIBLIOGRAPHY

Achebe, C., 1975. *An Image of Africa: Racism in Conrad's Heart of Darkness.* Amherst, University of Massachusetts.

Achebe, C., 2000. *Home and Exile.* Oxford: Oxford University Press.

Achebe, C., 2012. *There Was a Country: A Personal History of Biafra.* London: Penguin Books.

AfriForum, 2019. *AfriForum: Civil Rights Charter.* [Online]
Available at: https://afriforum.co.za/wp-content/uploads/2022/05/Civil-Rights-Charter-2019.pdf
[Accessed 9 October 2022].

Alexander, P. F., 1995. *Alan Paton: A Biography.* Oxford: Oxford University Press.

Alhadeff, V., 1976. *A Newspaper History of South Africa.* Charlottesville: University of Virginia.

Attwell, D., 1993. *South Africa and the Politics of Writing.* Berkely & Cape Town: University of California Press & David Philip.

BBC, 2015. *Angela Merkel attacked over crying refugee girl.* [Online]
Available at: https://www.bbc.com/news/world-europe-33555619
[Accessed 3 December 2020].

Biswas, S., 2015. *Was Mahatma Gandhi a Racist?* [Online]
Available at: https://www.bbc.com/news/world-asia-india-34265882
[Accessed 15 April 2020].

Boraine, A., 2014. *What's gone wrong: On the brink of a failed state.* Johannesburg: Jonathan Ball Publishers.

Bosman, H. C., 2003. *My Life and Opinions.* 3rd ed. Johannesburg: Human & Rousseau.

Bozzoli, B., 2019. *Politicsweb: The Janus face of African nationalism today.* [Online]
Available at: https://www.politicsweb.co.za/opinion/the-janus-face-of-african-nationalism-today
[Accessed 22 November 2022].

Bridgland, F., 1997. *Katiza's Journey: Beneath the Surface of South Africa's Shame.* London: Macmillan Publishers.

Buddha in Africa. 2019. [Film] Directed by Nicole Schafer. South Africa: Nicole Schafer.

Chipkin, I., 2020. *Daily Maverick: Let a thousand citizen blossoms bloom.* [Online]
Available at: https://www.dailymaverick.co.za/opinionista/2020-10-14-let-a-thousand-citizen-blossoms-bloom-kickstarting-and-policing-the-sa-economy/
[Accessed 8 October 2022].

Civilisation: A Personal View. 1969. [Film] Directed by Kenneth Clark. Britain: BBC.

Clarke, L., 2016. *Mazibuko rips into DA's white males.* [Online]
Available at: https://www.iol.co.za/news/politics/mazibuko-rips-into-das-white-males-1975033
[Accessed 25 November 2019].

Cronje, F., 2015. *The Rise or Fall of South Africa: Latest Scenarios.* Cape Town: Tafelberg.

Daily Maverick, 2021. *Daily Maverick: What Really Happened in Phoenix?* Johannesburg: Daily Maverick.

Denby, D., 1995. *The New Yorker: The Trouble with Heart of Darkness.* [Online]
Available at: https://www.newyorker.com/magazine/1995/11/06/the-trouble-with-heart-of-darkness
[Accessed 1 August 2022].

Dlamini, P., 2022. *'You know your party has a looting problem' – Steenhuisen to Ramaphosa.* [Online]
Available at: https://www.news24.com/citypress/news/you-know-your-party-has-a-looting-problem-steenhuisen-to-ramaphosa-20220426
[Accessed 18 July 2022].

Don Beck, C. C., 1996. *Spiral Dynamics.* Hoboken, New Jersey: Blackwell Publishing.

Du Preez, M., 2010. *Pale Native: Memories of a Renegade Reporter.* Cape Town: Zebra Press.

Dubow, S., 2019. *South Africa's Racist Founding Father Was Also a Human Rights Pioneer.* [Online]
Available at: https://www.nytimes.com/2019/05/18/opinion/jan-smuts-south-africa.html
[Accessed 21 September 2020].

Erasmus, D., 2021. *Outmanned, outgunned, outrun: Police commissioner Sitole admits SAPS' failings as SAHRC hearings continue.* [Online]
Available at: https://www.dailymaverick.co.za/article/2021-11-22-outmanned-outgunned-outrun-police-commissioner-sitole-admits-saps-failings-as-sahrc-hearings-continue/
[Accessed 23 December 2021].

Feinstein, A., 2009. *After the Party: Corruption, the ANC and South Africa's Uncertain Future.* London: Verso.

Ferguson, N., 2011. *Civilization.* London: Penguin Group.

Fukuyama, F., 2012. *The Origins of Political Order: From Prehuman Times to the French Revolution.* London: Profile Books.

Fukuyama, F., 2014. *Political Order and Political Decay: From the Industrial Revolution to the Globalisation of Democracy.* London: Profile Books.

Galal, S., 2022. *Distribution of languages spoken by individuals inside and outside of households in South Africa 2018.* [Online]
Available at: https://www.statista.com/statistics/1114302/distribution-of-languages-spoken-inside-and-outside-of-households-in-south-africa/
[Accessed 2 October 2022].

Gala, S., 2022. *Number of people employed in South Africa in Q4 2021, by industry.* [Online]
Available at: https://www.statista.com/statistics/1129815/number-of-people-employed-in-south-africa-by-industry/
[Accessed 23 September 2022].

Giliomee, H., 2016. *Historian Hermann Giliomee: An Autobiography.* Cape Town: Tafelberg.

Giliomee, H., 2016. *Politicsweb: Jan Smuts reconsidered.* [Online]
Available at: https://www.politicsweb.co.za/news-and-analysis/jan-smuts-reconsidered
[Accessed 8 October 2022].

Glbey, E., 1993. *The Lady: The Life and Times of Winnie Mandela.* Cape Town: Jonathan Cape.

Graves, C., 1981. *The Emergent, Cyclical, Double-Helix Model of the Adult Human Biopsychosocial Systems.* Boston: Graves.

Haffajee, F., 2015. *What If There Were No Whites in South Africa?* Johannesburg: Picador Africa.

Haidt, J., 2012. *The Righteous Mind: Why good people are divided by politics and religion.* New York City: Penguin Random House.

Harber, A., 2020. *So, For the Record.* Johannesburg: Jonathan Ball Publishers.

Hopkins, A., 1992. *Some Sort of a Job: My Life with Alan Paton.* Cape Town: Penguin.

Integral African Conference, 2020. *Integral African Conference.* [Online]
Available at: https://integralafricanconference.com/about-main/
[Accessed 1 September 2022].

International Monetary Fund, 2021. *Six Charts Show the Challenge Faced by Sub-Saharan Africa.* [Online]
Available at: https://www.imf.org/en/News/Articles/2021/04/12/na041521-six-charts-show-the-challenges-faced-by-sub-saharan-africa
[Accessed 12 December 2021].

IOL, 2019. *Zille ruffles feathers with controversial remark on promoting black people in DA.* [Online]
Available at: https://www.iol.co.za/news/politics/zille-ruffles-feathers-with-controversial-remark-on-promoting-black-people-in-da-24332532
[Accessed 12 April 2021].

Johnson, R. W., 2015. *How Long Will South Africa Survive?* Cape Town: Jonathan Ball.

Jonas, M., 2019. *After Dawn: Hope After State Capture.* Cape Town: Picador Africa.

Kane-Berman, R. E. &. J., 2000. *Political Correctness in South Africa.* Johannesbuurg: South African Institute of Race Relations & Friedrich Naumann Foundation.

Laband, J., 2020. *The Land Wars.* Cape Town: Penguin Random House.

Lean on Me. 1989. [Film] Directed by John G. Avildsen. United States: Warner Bros.

Loury, G., 2022. *The Glenn Show: Matters of Race, Matters of Mind.* [Online]
Available at: https://www.youtube.com/watch?v=KLfm8MBiPOQ
[Accessed 19 July 2022].

Louvish, S., 2002. *That lad will go far!* [Online]
Available at: https://www.theguardian.com/film/2002/dec/06/artsfeatures.popandrock
[Accessed 5 June 2020].

Maclean, C. R. & Gray, S., 1996. *The Natal Papers of John Ross.* Scottsville: University of KwaZulu-Natal Press.

Makinana, A., 2014. *Ramphele's move to DA will remove race card, says Zille.* [Online]
Available at: https://mg.co.za/article/2014-01-28-rampheles-move-to-da-will-remove-race-card-says-zille/
[Accessed 23 July 2021].

Malan, R., 2021. *How 'equity' ideology plunged South Africa into inequality and chaos.* [Online]
Available at: https://nypost.com/2021/07/19/how-equity-ideology-plunged-south-africa-into-inequality-and-chaos/
[Accessed 19 January 2022].

Mangcu, X., 2013. *Biko: A Life.* London: IB Tauris.

Marks, S., 2001. White Masculinity: Jan Smuts, Race and the South African War. *Proceedings of the British Academy,* Volume III, pp. 199-223.

Mashaba, H., 2019. *PART ONE: I am gravely concerned that the DA I signed up to, is no longer the DA that has emerged out of this weekend's Federal Council.* [Online]
Available at: https://twitter.com/HermanMashaba/status/1186210421814026240?ref_src=twsrc%5Etfw%7Ctwcamp%5Etweetembed%7Ctwterm%5E1186210421814026240%7Ctwgr%5E%7Ctwcon%5Es1_&ref_url=https%3A%2F%2Fwww.citizen.co.za%2Fnews%2Fsouth-africa%2Fpolitics%2F2193509%2Fmashaba-resi
[Accessed 8 October 2022].

Mattison, J., 2015. *God, Spies and Lies.* Cape Town: Pan Macmillan.

McGilchrist, I., 2009. *The Master and His Emissary: The Divided Brain and the Making of the Western World.* Boston: Yale University Press.

Meis, M., 2016. *The New Yorker: The Seductive Enthusiasm of Kenneth Clark's Civilisation.* [Online]
Available at: https://www.newyorker.com/books/page-turner/the-seductive-enthusiasm-of-kenneth-clarks-civilisationhttps://www.newyorker.com/books/page-turner/the-seductive-enthusiasm-of-kenneth-clarks-civilisation
[Accessed 17 August 2021].

Moya, N., 2006. *100% Zuluboy.* [Online]
Available at: https://mg.co.za/article/2006-04-06-100-zuluboy/
[Accessed 2 April 2020].

Msimang, P., 2018. Non-racialism isn't in the future of South Africa: towards a pessimistic view of race in South Africa. *Transformation: Critical Perspectives on Southern Africa 96(1)*, https://www.researchgate.net/publication/324685994_Non-racialism_isn't_in_the_future_of_South_Africa_towards_a_pessimistic_view_of_race_in_South_Africa

Msimang, S., 2018. *The Resurrection of Winnie Mandela.* Cape Town: Jonathan Ball.

news24, 2014. *Mazibuko would have lost position - Zille.* [Online]
Available at: https://www.news24.com/News24/mazibuko-would-have-lost-position-zille-20140514
[Accessed 29 April 2021].

news24, 2014. *Ramphele quits party politics.* [Online]
Available at: https://www.news24.com/News24/Ramphele-quits-party-politics-20140708
[Accessed 1 October 2022].

news24, 2019. *FULL STATEMENT | Mmusi Maimane's final words as opposition leader: 'DA not suited to build One South Africa for All'.* [Online]
Available at: https://www.news24.com/news24/SouthAfrica/News/in-full-mmusi-maimanes-final-words-as-opposition-leader-da-not-suited-to-build-one-south-africa-for-all-20191023

Nguyen, M.-N., 2021. *Number of employed people in Vietnam in 2020, by industry.* [Online]
Available at: https://www.statista.com/statistics/615802/employment-by-industry-vietnam/#:~:text=In%202020%2C%20almost%2017.73%20million,of%20employed%20population%20that%20year.
[Accessed 6 November 2021].

Nwaubani, A., 2020. *Remembering Nigeria's Biafra war that many prefer to forget.* [Online]
Available at: https://www.bbc.com/news/world-africa-51094093
[Accessed 28 November 2020].

Obioma, C., 2016. *Why Black People Must Help Africa Develop.* [Online]
Available at: https://foreignpolicy.com/2016/08/09/why-black-people-must-help-africa-develop-racism-pan-africanism/
[Accessed 16 July 2019].

Orwell, G., 2017. *Literary Hub: George Orwell's 1940 Review of Mein Kampf.* [Online]
Available at: https://bookmarks.reviews/george-orwells-1940-review-of-mein-kampf/
[Accessed 8 October 2022].

Paton, A., 1948. *Cry, the Beloved Country.* New York: Charles Scribner's Sons.

Paton, A., 1986. *Towards the Mountain.* Harmondsworth: Penguin Books.

Pauw, J., 2017. *The President's Keepers: Those Keeping Zuma in Power and Out of Prison.* Cape Town: Tafelberg.

Plaatje, S. T., 2007. *Native Life in South Africa: Before and Since the European War and the Boer Rebellion.* Johannesburg: Pan Macmillan.

Putnam, R. D., 2000. *Bowling Alone: The Collapse and Revival of American Community.* New York: Simon & Schuster.

Richard, 2020. *The Rise or Fall of South Africa: Latest Scenarios.* [Online]
Available at: https://www.amazon.com/Rise-Fall-South-Africa-scenarios/dp/0624091384#customerReviews
[Accessed 17 June 2021].

SA news, 2022. *sanews.gov.za: Public, private sectors play key role in employment, growth.* [Online]
Available at: https://www.sanews.gov.za/south-africa/public-private-sectors-play-key-role-employment-growth
[Accessed 5 October 2022].

SAHO, 2022. *South African History Online: Durban Timeline 1497-1990.* [Online]
Available at: https://www.sahistory.org.za/article/durban-timeline-1497-1990
[Accessed 23 November 2022].

Sandel, M., 2022. *Michael Sandel quotes.* [Online]
Available at: https://www.brainyquote.com/authors/michael-sandel-quotes
[Accessed 16 November 2022].

SAPA, 1997. *Justice.gov.za/trc/media: Winnie handed over gun to murder Asvat, says killer.* [Online]
Available at: https://www.justice.gov.za/trc/media/1997/9712/s971201j.htm
[Accessed 23 July 2020].

Shweder, R., Much, N., Mahapatra, M. & Park, L., 1997. The 'Big Three' of Morality (Autonomy, Community, Divinity) and the 'Big Three' Explanations of Suffering. *Morality and Health,* pp. 119-169.

Smuts, J., 1927. *Holism and Evolution.* 2nd ed. London: Macmillan & Co.

Smuts, J. C., 1973. *Walt Whitman: A Study in the Evolution of Personality.* Detroit: Wayne State University Press.

Soudien, C., 2012. Neville Alexander: political philosopher (1936 - 2012). *S Afr J Sci. 2012;108(11/12), Art. #1450, 2 pages.,* pp. Art. #1450, 2 pages. (http://www.scielo.org.za/pdf/sajs/v108n11-12/09.pdf).

South African Democracy Educaton Trust, 2020. *The Road to South Africa, Volume 8, Part 1.* Pretoria: Unisa Press.

South African History Online, 2019. *Abram Ramothibi Onkgopotse Tiro.* [Online]
Available at: https://www.sahistory.org.za/people/abram-ramothibi-onkgopotse-tiro
[Accessed 07 July 2022].

South African History Online, 2019. *South African Student Organisation (SASO).* [Online]
Available at: https://www.sahistory.org.za/article/south-african-student-organisation-saso
[Accessed 11 December 2020].

Statista, 2021. *The population of South Africa in 2021, in ethnic groups.* [Online]
Available at: https://www.statista.com/statistics/1116076/total-population-of-south-africa-by-population-group/
[Accessed 10 September 2022].

Stewart, J. P., 2012. *IPE.com: I know it when I see it.* [Online]
Available at: https://www.ipe.com/i-know-it-when-i-see-it/48642.
article#:~:text=In%201964%2C%20Justice%20Potter%20
Stewart,it%20when%20I%20see%20it.%E2%80%9D
[Accessed 25 July 2022].

The Citizen, 2019. *Mashaba resigns as Johannesburg mayor following Zille's return.* [Online]
Available at: https://www.citizen.co.za/
news/south-africa/politics/2193509/
mashaba-resigns-as-johannesburg-mayor-following-zilles-return/

The Economist, 2021. *Where does South Africa go from here?* [Online]
Available at: https://www.economist.
com/middle-east-and-africa/2021/07/24/
where-does-south-africa-go-from-here

The Economist, 2021. *Special Report.* [Online]
Available at: https://www.economist.com/special-report/2021/05/14/what-it-means-to-be-an-american
[Accessed 17 June 2022].

The Glenn Show, 2022. *YouTube: Reclaiming Black Dignity: Glenn Loury and Sam Harris.* [Online]
[Accessed 19 07 2022].

The Guardian, 2002. *Book club.* [Online]
Available at: https://www.theguardian.com/books/2002/jun/01/
featuresreviews.guardianreview31
[Accessed 10 February 2020].

Tribe magazine, Muna Ndlovu, 2022. *Tribe.* Cape Town: Reignmakers.

Waking Up with Sam Harris, 2018. *Waking up with Sam Harris #73 - Forbidden Knowledge with Charles Murray [Video].* [Online]
Available at: https://www.youtube.com/watch?v=dv0SFuArjGI
[Accessed 19 07 2022].

Whitfield, B., 2020. *financialmail: Bruce Whitfield: An open letter to my fund manager*. [Online]
Available at: https://www.businesslive.co.za/fm/opinion/2020-07-17-bruce-whitfield-an-open-letter-to-my-fund-manager/
[Accessed 23 November 2022].

Wikipedia, 2022. *Brian Molefe*. [Online]
Available at: https://en.wikipedia.org/wiki/Brian_Molefe
[Accessed 7 June 2022].

Wikipedia, 2020. *Wikipedia: Xhosa Wars*. [Online]
Available at: https://en.wikipedia.org/wiki/Xhosa_Wars#Sixth_war_(1834%E2%80%931836)
[Accessed 10 November 2020].

Wikipedia, 2022. *Cry, the Beloved Country* (1951 film). [Online]
Available at: https://en.wikipedia.org/wiki/Cry,_the_Beloved_Country_(1951_film)
[Accessed 20 July 2022].

Wikipedia, 2022. *Durban riots*. [Online]
Available at: https://en.wikipedia.org/wiki/Durban_riots#cite_note-4
[Accessed 15 January 2021].

Willan, B., 2018. *Sol Plaatje*. Cape Town: Jacana Media.

Woods, D., 1978. *Biko*. London: Paddington Press Ltd.

York, G., 2016. *Libertarian Herman Mashaba elected mayor of Johannesburg*. [Online]
Available at: https://www.theglobeandmail.com/news/world/libertarian-herman-mashaba-elected-mayor-of-johannesburg/article31942363/
[Accessed 18 March 2020].

Zille, H., 2021. *Facebook: 15 May 2021*. [Online]
Available at: https://web.facebook.com/HelenZille/?_rdc=1&_rdr
[Accessed 23 November 2022].

Zille, H., 2017. *Tweet*. [Online]
Available at: https://twitter.com/helenzille/status/947390593818341377
[Accessed 12 March 2020].